ROOKIE COACHES SOFTBALL GUIDE

American Coaching Effectiveness Program

Leisure Press
Champaign, Illinois

Library of Congress Cataloging-in-Publication Data

Rookie coaches softball guide / American Coaching Effectiveness Program.
     p.   cm.
     ISBN 0-88011-418-5
     1. Softball for children—Coaching.   2. Softball—Coaching.
I. American Coaching Effectiveness Program.
GV881.4.C6R66   1992
796.357'8—dc20   91-42386
                                                                          CIP

ISBN: 0-88011-418-5

Figure 6.2 is from *Coaching Softball Effectively* (p. 9) by Steven D. Houseworth. Copyright 1985 by Human Kinetics Publishers, Inc. Reprinted by permission. Figures 8.1-8.22 are from *The Softball Handbook* (pp. 100-111) by Susan Craig and Ken Johnson. Copyright 1985 by Leisure Press. Reprinted by permission.

Developmental Editor: Ted Miller
Managing Editors: Julia Anderson, Jan Colarusso Seeley
Softball Consultants: Cindy Bristow, Amateur Softball Association
                          Susan Craig and Ken Johnson, University
                          of New Mexico
Assistant Editor: Elizabeth Bridgett
Copyeditor: Jane Bowers
Proofreaders: Dawn Levy, Kari Nelson
Production Director: Ernie Noa
Typesetter: Ruby Zimmerman
Text Design: Keith Blomberg
Text Layout: Denise Lowry
Cover Design: Jack Davis
Cover Photo: John Kilroy/Photo Concepts
Interior Art: Keith Blomberg, Timothy Stiles, Gretchen Walters
Printer: United Graphics

Leisure Press books are available at special discounts for bulk purchase for sales promotions, premiums, fund-raising, or educational use. Special editions or book excerpts can also be created to specification. For details, contact the Special Sales Manager at Leisure Press.

Printed in the United States of America

10 9 8 7 6 5 4 3 2 1

Leisure Press
A Division of Human Kinetics Publishers, Inc.
Box 5076, Champaign, IL 61825-5076
1-800-747-4457

Canada Office:
Human Kinetics Publishers, Inc.
P.O. Box 2503, Windsor, ON N8Y 4S2
1-800-465-7301 (in Canada only)

Europe Office:
Human Kinetics Publishers (Europe) Ltd.
P.O. Box IW14
Leeds LS16 6TR
England
0532-781708

Contents

Welcome to Coaching!

oaching young people is an exciting way to be involved in sport. But it isn't easy. Some coaches are overwhelmed by the responsibilities involved in helping athletes through their early sport experiences. And that's not surprising, because coaching youngsters requires more than putting out the bats and balls and letting them play. It involves preparing them physically and mentally to compete effectively, fairly, and safely in their sport and providing them with a positive role model.

This book will help you meet these challenges *and* experience the many rewards of coaching young athletes. We call it the *Rookie Coaches Softball Guide* because it is intended for adults with little or no formal preparation in coaching softball. In this *Rookie Guide* you'll learn how to apply general coaching principles in youth softball. And you'll also know how to teach the rules, skills, and strategies of softball to kids after you read the last three units of the book, which were contributed by Susan Craig and Ken Johnson, veteran University of New Mexico softball coaches.

This book also serves as a text for the American Coaching Effectiveness Program's (ACEP) Rookie Coaches Course. If you would like more information about the Rookie

Coaches Course, or any of the other courses ACEP offers, please contact us at

ACEP
Box 5076
Champaign, IL 61825-5076
1-800-747-4457

Good Coaching!

UNIT
1

Who, Me . . . a Coach?

If you're like most youth league coaches, you were recruited from the ranks of concerned parents, sport enthusiasts, or community volunteers. And, like many rookie *and* veteran coaches, you probably have had little formal instruction on how to coach. But when the call went out for coaches to assist with the local youth softball program, you answered because you like children, enjoy softball, are community-minded, and perhaps are interested in starting a coaching career.

I Want to Help, But . . .

Your initial coaching assignment may be difficult. Like many volunteers, you may not know everything there is to know about softball, nor about how to work with children between the ages of 6 and 14. Relax. This *Rookie Coaches Softball Guide* will help you learn the basics for coaching softball effectively. In the coming pages you will find the answers to such common questions as the following:

- What tools do I need to be a good coach?

- How can I best communicate with my players?
- How do I go about teaching sport skills?
- What can I do to promote safety?
- What actions do I take when someone is injured?
- What are the basic rules, skills, and strategies of softball?
- What practice drills will improve my players' softball skills?

Before answering these questions, let's take a look at what's involved in being a coach.

Am I a Parent or a Coach?

Many coaches are parents, but the two roles should not be confused. As a parent you are responsible only to yourself and your child; as a coach you are responsible to the organization, all the players on the team (including your child), their parents, and yourself.

When you assume these additional responsibilities as a coach, your child may not understand why you behave differently on the softball field than you do at home. To avoid problems, take the following steps when coaching your child:

- Ask your child if he or she wants you to coach the team.
- Explain why you wish to be involved with the team.
- Discuss with your child your new responsibilities and how they will affect your relationship when coaching.
- Limit your "coach" behavior to those times when you are in a coaching role.
- Avoid parenting during practice or game situations to keep your role clear in your child's mind.
- Reaffirm your love for your child irrespective of his or her performance on the softball diamond.

What Are My Responsibilities as a Coach?

A coach assumes the responsibility of doing everything possible to ensure that the youngsters on his or her team will have an enjoyable and safe sporting experience while they learn sport skills. If you're ever in doubt about your approach, remind yourself that "fun and fundamentals" are most important.

Provide an Enjoyable Experience

Softball should be fun. Even if nothing else is accomplished, make certain your players

have fun. Take the fun out of sport and you'll take the kids out of sport.

Children enter sport for a number of reasons (e.g., to meet and play with other children, to develop physically, to learn skills), but their major objective is to have fun. Help them satisfy this goal by injecting humor and variety into your practices. Also, make games nonthreatening, festive experiences for your players. Such an approach will increase their desire for future participation, which should be the primary goal of youth sport. Unit 2 will help you learn how to satisfy your players' yearning for fun and keep winning in perspective. And, Unit 3 will describe how to communicate this perspective effectively to them.

Provide a Safe Experience

You are responsible for planning and teaching activities in such a way that the progression between activities minimizes risks (see Units 4 and 5). You also must ensure that the facility at which your team practices and plays, and the equipment team members use, are free of hazards. Finally, you need to protect yourself from any legal liability issues that might arise from your involvement as a coach. Unit 5 will help you take the appropriate precautions.

Teach Basic Softball Skills

In becoming a coach, you take on the role of educator. You must teach your players the fundamental skills and strategies necessary for success in softball. That means that you need to "go to school." You'll also find that you are better able to teach the softball skills and strategies you do know if you plan your practices. Unit 4 of this manual provides guidelines for effective practice planning.

If you don't know the basics of softball now, you can learn them by reading the second half of this manual. And even if you know softball as a player, do you know how to teach it? This book will help you get started. Furthermore, many valuable softball books are available, including those offered by Human Kinetics Publishers. See the listing of books in the back of this book or call 1-800-747-4457 for more information.

Where Do I Get Help?

Veteran coaches in your league are an especially good source of information and assistance. You can also learn a great deal by observing local high school coaches in practices and games. You might even ask a few of the coaches you respect most to lend a hand with a couple of your practices. These coaches have experienced the same emotions and concerns you are facing; their advice and feedback can be invaluable as you work through your first season of coaching.

You can get additional help by attending softball coaching clinics, reading softball publications, and studying instructional videos. Finally, the American Coaching Effectiveness Program and the following national organizations will assist you in obtaining more softball coaching information.

Amateur Softball Association
  2801 NE 50th Street
  Oklahoma City, OK 73111
  (405) 424-5266
  (800)-44-Coach

National Softball Coaches Association
  c/o Kim Vance, Executive Director
  University of Chicago
  5640 South University
  Chicago, IL 60637
  (312) 702-9556

Softball Canada
  1600 James Naismith Drive
  Gloucester, Ontario
  Canada K1B 5N4
  (613) 748-5706

Coaching softball is a rewarding experience. And, just as you want your players to learn and practice to be the best they can be, learn all you can about coaching so you can be the best softball coach you can be.

UNIT 2

What Tools Do I Need to Coach?

Have you purchased the traditional coaching tools—things like whistles, coaching clothes, baseball shoes, and a clipboard? They'll help you coach, but to be a successful coach you'll need five other *tools* that cannot be bought. These tools are available only through self-examination and hard work, but they're easy to remember with the acronym COACH:

C—Comprehension
O—Outlook
A—Affection
C—Character
H—Humor

Comprehension

Comprehension of the rules, skills, and tactics of softball is required. It is essential that you understand the basic elements of the sport. To assist you in learning about the game, the last three units of this guide describe the rules, skills, and tactics of softball, and suggest how to plan for the season and individual practices. In the softball-specific section of this guide, you'll also find a variety of drills to use in developing young players' softball skills.

To improve your comprehension of softball, take the following steps:

- Read the sport-specific section of this book.
- Consider reading other softball coaching books, including those available from ACEP (see p. 76 to order).
- Contact any of the organizations listed on pages 3 and 4.
- Attend softball coaches' clinics.
- Talk with other, more experienced softball coaches.
- Observe local college, high school, and youth softball games.

In addition to having softball knowledge, you must implement proper training and safety methods so that your players can participate with little risk of injury. Even then, sport injuries will occur. And, more often than not, you'll be the first person responding to your players' injuries. Therefore, make sure you understand the basic emergency care procedures described in Unit 5. In that unit you will also read about how to handle more serious sport injury situations.

Outlook

This coaching tool refers to your perspective and goals—what you are seeking as a coach. The most common coaching objectives are (a) to have fun, (b) to help players develop their physical, mental, and social skills, and (c) to win. Thus *outlook* involves the priorities you set, your planning, and your vision for the future.

To work successfully with children in a sport setting, you must have your priorities in order. In just what order do you rank the importance of fun, development, and winning?

Answer the following questions to examine your objectives.

Of which situation would you be most proud?

a. Knowing that each participant enjoyed playing softball
b. Seeing that all players improved their softball skills
c. Winning the league championship

Which statement best reflects your thoughts about sport?

a. If it isn't fun, don't do it.
b. Everyone should learn something every day.
c. Sport isn't fun if you don't win.

How would you like your players to remember you?

a. As a coach who was fun to play for
b. As a coach who provided a good base of fundamental skills
c. As a coach who had a winning record

Which would you most like to hear a parent of a child on your team say?

a. Karen really had a good time playing softball this year.

b. Jerry learned some important lessons playing softball this year.

c. Margie played on the first-place softball team this year.

Which of the following would be the most rewarding moment of your season?

a. Having your team not want to stop playing even after practice is over

b. Observing your players finally master the skill of fielding ground balls

c. Winning the league championship

Look over your answers. If you most often selected "a" responses, then having fun is most important to you. A majority of "b" answers suggests that skill development is what attracts you to coaching. And if "c" was your most frequent response, winning is tops on your list of coaching priorities.

Most coaches say fun and development are more important, but when actually coaching, some coaches emphasize—indeed overemphasize—winning. You too will face situations that challenge you to keep winning in its proper perspective. During such moments you'll have to choose between emphasizing your players' development and winning. If your priorities are in order, your players' well-being will take precedence over your team's win-loss record every time.

Take the following actions to better define your outlook:

- Determine your priorities for the season.
- Prepare for situations that challenge your priorities.
- Set goals for yourself and your players that are consistent with those priorities.
- Plan how you and your players can best attain those goals.
- Review your goals frequently to be sure that you are staying on track.

It is particularly important for coaches to permit all young athletes to participate. Each youngster should have an opportunity to develop skills and have fun—even if it means sacrificing a win or two during the season. After all, wouldn't you prefer losing a couple of games to losing a couple of players' interest in softball?

Remember that the challenge and joy of sport is experienced through *striving to win*, not through winning itself. Players who aren't allowed off the bench are denied the opportunity to strive to win. And herein lies the irony: A coach who allows all of his or her players to participate and develop skills will, in the end, come out on top.

ACEP has a motto that will help you keep your outlook in the best interest of the kids on your team. It summarizes in four words all you need to remember when establishing your coaching priorities:

Athletes First, Winning Second

This motto recognizes that striving to win is an important, even vital part of sport. But it emphatically states that no efforts in striving to win should be made at the expense of athletes' well-being, development, and enjoyment.

Affection

This is another vital *tool* you will want to have in your coaching kit: a genuine concern for the young people you coach. *Affection* involves having a love for children, a desire to share with them your love and knowledge of sport, and the patience and understanding that allows each individual playing for you to grow from her or his involvement in softball.

Successful coaches have a real concern for the health and welfare of their players. They care that each child on the team has an enjoyable and successful experience. They have a strong desire to work with children and be involved in their growth. And they have the patience to work with those who are slower to learn or less capable of performing. If you have such qualities or are willing to work hard to develop them, then you have the affection necessary to coach young athletes.

There are many ways to demonstrate your affection and patience, including the following:

- Make an effort to get to know each player on your team.

- Treat each player as an individual.
- Empathize with players' trying to learn new and difficult softball skills.
- Treat players as you would like to be treated under similar circumstances.
- Be in control of your emotions.
- Show your enthusiasm for being involved with your team.
- Keep an upbeat and positive tone in all of your communications.

Character

Youngsters learn by listening to what adults say. But they learn even more by watching the behaviors of certain important individuals. As a coach, you are likely to be a significant figure in the lives of your players. Will you be a good role model?

Having good *character* means modeling appropriate behaviors for sport and life. That means more than just saying the right things. What you say and what you do must match. There is no place in coaching for the "Do as I say, not as I do" philosophy. Be in control before, during, and after all games and practices. And don't be afraid to admit that you were wrong. No one is perfect!

Consider the following steps to being a good role model:

- Take stock of your strengths and weaknesses.
- Build on your strengths.
- Set goals for yourself to improve upon those areas you would not like to see mimicked.
- If you slip up, apologize to your team and to yourself. You'll do better next time.

Humor

Humor is often overlooked as a coaching tool. For our use it means having the ability to laugh *at* yourself and *with* your players during practices and games. Nothing helps balance the tone of a serious, skill-learning session like a chuckle or two. And a sense of humor puts in perspective the many mistakes your young players will make. So don't get upset over each miscue or respond negatively to erring players. Allow your players and yourself to enjoy the "ups," and don't dwell on the "downs."

Here are some tips for injecting humor into your practices:

- Make practices fun by including a variety of activities.
- Keep all players involved in practice drills.
- Consider laughter by your players a sign of enjoyment, not a lack of discipline.
- Smile!

Where Do You Stand?

To take stock of your "coaching tool kit," rank yourself on each of the three questions concerning the five coaching tools. Simply circle the number that best describes your *present* status on each item.

Not at all		Somewhat		Very much so
1	2	3	4	5

Comprehension

1. Could you explain the rules of softball to other parents without studying for a long time?   1 2 3 4 5
2. Do you know how to organize and conduct safe softball practices?   1 2 3 4 5
3. Do you know how to provide first aid for most common, minor sport injuries?   1 2 3 4 5

Comprehension Score: _____

Outlook

4. Do you have winning in its proper perspective when you coach?   1 2 3 4 5
5. Do you plan for every meeting, practice, and game?   1 2 3 4 5
6. Do you have a vision of what you want your players to be able to do by the end of the season?   1 2 3 4 5

Outlook Score: _____

Affection

7. Do you enjoy working with children?   1 2 3 4 5
8. Are you patient with youngsters learning new skills?   1 2 3 4 5
9. Are you able to show your players that you care?   1 2 3 4 5

Affection Score: _____

Character

10. Are your words consistent with your behavior?   1 2 3 4 5
11. Are you a good model for your players?   1 2 3 4 5
12. Do you keep negative emotions under control before, during, and after games?   1 2 3 4 5

Character Score: _____

Humor

13. Do you usually smile at your players?   1 2 3 4 5
14. Are your practices fun?   1 2 3 4 5
15. Are you able to laugh at your mistakes?   1 2 3 4 5

Humor Score: _____

If you scored 9 or less on any of the coaching tools, be sure to reread those sections carefully. And even if you scored 15 on each tool, don't be complacent. Keep learning! Then you'll be well-equipped with the tools you need to coach young athletes.

UNIT 3

How Should I Communicate With My Players?

EVERYBODY GOT THAT?

Now you know the tools needed to COACH: Comprehension, Outlook, Affection, Character, and Humor are essential for effective coaching. Without them, you'd have a difficult time getting started. But none of these tools will work if you don't know how to use them with your athletes—that requires skillful communication. This unit examines what communication is and how you can become a more effective communicator-coach.

What's Involved in Communication?

Coaches often believe that communication involves only instructing players to do something, but these verbal commands are a very small part of the communication process.

More than half of what is communicated in a message is nonverbal. So when you are coaching, remember that "actions speak louder than words."

Communication in its simplest form involves two people: a *sender* and a *receiver*. The sender can transmit the message verbally, through facial expression, and/or via body language. Once the message is sent, the receiver must try to determine the meaning of the message. A receiver who fails to attend or listen will miss part, if not all, of the message.

How Can I Send More Effective Messages?

Young athletes often have little understanding of the rules and skills of softball, and they probably have even less confidence in playing it. So they need accurate, understandable, and supportive messages to help them along. That's why it's so important for you to send verbal and nonverbal messages effectively.

Verbal Messages

The adage "Sticks and stones may break my bones, but words will never hurt me" isn't true. Spoken words can have a strong and long-lasting effect. And coaches' words are particularly influential, because youngsters place great importance on what coaches say. Therefore, whether you are correcting a misbehavior, teaching a player how to hit the ball, or praising a player for good effort,

- *be positive, but honest;*
- *state it clearly and simply;*
- *say it loud enough and say it again; and*
- *send consistent messages.*

Be Positive, but Honest

Nothing turns people off like hearing someone nag all the time. Young athletes are similarly discouraged by a coach who gripes constantly. The players on your team need encouragement because many of them

doubt their ability to play softball. So *look* for and *tell* your players what they did well.

On the other hand, don't cover up poor or incorrect play with rosy words of praise. Kids know all too well when they've made a mistake, and no cheerfully expressed cliché can undo their errors. And if you fail to acknowledge players' errors, your athletes will think you are a phony.

A good way to handle situations in which you have identified and must correct improper technique is to serve your players a "compliment sandwich."

1. Point out what the athlete did correctly.
2. Let the player know what was incorrect in the performance and instruct him or her how to correct it.
3. Encourage the player by reemphasizing what he or she did well.

State It Clearly and Simply

Positive and honest messages are good, but only if expressed directly and in words your players understand. "Beating around the bush" is an ineffective and inefficient way to send verbal messages. If you ramble, your players will miss the point of your message and probably lose interest. Here are some tips for saying things clearly:

- Organize your thoughts before speaking to your athletes.
- Explain things thoroughly, but don't bore them with long-winded monologues.
- Use language that your players can understand. However, avoid trying to be "hip" by using their age group's slang.

Say It Loud Enough and Say It Again

A large playing field filled with players scattered about can make communication difficult. So talk to your team in a voice that all members can hear and interpret. It's okay, in fact appropriate, to soften your voice when speaking to a player individually about a personal problem. But most of the time your messages will be for all your players to hear; so make sure they can! A word of caution, however: Don't dominate the setting with a booming voice that intimidates players or detracts attention from their performances.

Sometimes what you say, even if stated loud and clear, won't sink in the first time. This may be particularly true with young athletes hearing words they don't understand. To avoid boring repetition but still get your message across, say the same thing in a slightly different way. For instance, you might first tell your players, "Get down on the ball." Then, soon thereafter, remind them to "Move in front of the ball, bend your knees, drop the hips, and put the back of the

glove on the ground to make sure you catch ground balls." The second message may get through to some players who did not understand or missed it the first time around.

Send Consistent Messages

People often say things in a way that implies a different message. For example, a touch of sarcasm added to the words "way to go" sends an entirely different message than the words themselves suggest. It is essential that you avoid sending such mixed messages. Keep the tone of your voice consistent with the words you use. And don't say something one day and contradict it the next; players will get confused.

Nonverbal Messages

Just as you should be consistent in the tone of voice and words you use, you should also keep your verbal and nonverbal messages consistent. An extreme example of failing to do this would be shaking your head, indicating disapproval, while at the same time telling a player "nice try." Which is the player to believe, your gesture or your words?

Messages can be sent nonverbally in a number of ways. Surely, you'll be motioning players where to position themselves in the field and signaling instructions to batters. These and other forms of body language, as well as facial expressions, can help you communicate when you coach.

Body Language

Your players will soon let you know if your fielding and hitting signals are effective. But what about your other body language? How would your players think you felt if you came to practice slouched over, with head down and shoulders slumped? Tired? Bored? Unhappy? How would they think you felt if you watched them during a contest with your hands on your hips, jaws clenched, and face reddened? Upset with them? Disgusted at an official? Mad at a fan? Probably some or all of these things would enter your players' minds. That's why you should carry yourself in a pleasant, confident, and vigorous manner. Such a posture not only projects happiness with your coaching role, it also provides a good example for young players who may model your behavior.

Physical contact can also be a very important use of body language. A handshake, a pat on the head, an arm around the shoulder, and even a big hug are effective ways of showing approval, concern, affection, and joy to your players. Youngsters are especially in need of this type of nonverbal message. Keep within the obvious moral and legal limits, but don't be reluctant to touch your players and send a message that can only truly be expressed in that way.

Facial Expressions

The look on a person's face is the quickest clue to what he or she thinks or feels. Your players know this, so they will study your face, looking for any sign that will tell them more than the words you say. Don't try to fool them by putting on a happy or blank "mask." They'll see through it, and you'll lose credibility.

Serious, stone-faced expressions are no help to kids who need cues as to how they are performing. They will just assume you're unhappy or disinterested. So don't be afraid to smile. A smile from a coach can boost the confidence of an unsure young athlete. Plus, a smile lets your players know that you are happy coaching them. But don't overdo it, because then your players won't be able to tell when you are genuinely pleased by something they've done or when you are just "putting on" a smiling face.

How Can I Improve My Receiving Skills?

Now let's examine the other half of the communication process—receiving messages. Too often people are very good senders and very poor receivers of messages; they seem to naturally enjoy hearing themselves talk more than listening to others. As a coach of young athletes, you must receive their verbal and nonverbal messages effectively. You can be a better receiver of your players' messages if you are willing to read about the

keys to receiving messages and then make a strong effort to use them with your players. You'll be surprised what you've been missing.

Attention!

First you must pay attention; you must want to hear what others have to communicate to you. That's not always easy when you're busy coaching and have many things competing for your attention. But in one-to-one or team meetings with players, you must really focus on what they are telling you, both verbally and nonverbally. Not only will such focused attention help you catch every word they say, but you'll also notice their mood and physical state, and you'll get an idea of their feelings toward you and other players on the team.

Listen CARE-FULLY

How we receive messages from others, perhaps more than anything else we do, demonstrates how much we care for the sender and what that person has to tell us. If you care little for your players or have little regard for what they have to say, it will show in how you attend and listen to them. Check yourself. Do you find your mind wandering to what you are going to do after practice while one of your players is talking to you? Do you frequently have to ask your players, "What did you say?" If so, you need to work on your attending and listening skills. If you find that you're missing the messages your players send, perhaps the most critical question you should ask yourself is this: Do I care?

How Do I Put It All Together?

So far we've discussed separately the sending and receiving of messages. But we all know that senders and receivers switch roles several times during an interaction. One person initiates a communication by sending a message to another person who then receives the message. The receiver then switches roles and becomes the sender by responding to the person who sent the initial message. These verbal and nonverbal responses are called *feedback*.

Your players will be looking to you for feedback all the time. They will want to know how you think they are performing, what you think of their ideas, and whether their efforts please you. *How you respond* will strongly affect your players. So let's take a look at a few general types of feedback and examine their possible effects.

Providing Instructions

With young players, much of your feedback will involve answering questions about how to play softball. Your instructive responses to these questions should include both verbal and nonverbal feedback. The following are suggestions for giving instructional feedback:

- Keep verbal instructions simple and concise.
- Use demonstrations to provide nonverbal instructional feedback (see Unit 4).
- Walk players through the skill, or use a slow-motion demonstration if they are having trouble learning.

Correcting Errors

When your players perform incorrectly, you need to provide informative feedback to correct the error—and the sooner the better. And when you do correct errors, keep in mind these two principles: Use negative criticism sparingly, and keep calm.

Use Negative Criticism Sparingly

Although you may need to punish players for horseplay or dangerous activities by scolding or temporarily removing them from activity, avoid reprimanding players for performance errors. Admonishing players for honest mistakes makes them afraid to even try. Nothing ruins a youngster's enjoyment of softball more than a coach who harps on every miscue. So instead, correct your players by using the positive approach. They'll enjoy playing more and you'll enjoy coaching more.

Keep Calm

Don't fly off the handle when your players make mistakes. Remember, you're coaching young and inexperienced players, not pros. You'll therefore see more incorrect than correct technique, and probably have more discipline problems than you expect. But throwing a tantrum over each error or misbehavior will only inhibit them or suggest to them the wrong kind of behavior to model. Let your players know that mistakes aren't the end of the world; and, stay cool!

Giving Positive Feedback

Praising players when they have performed or behaved well is an effective way of getting them to repeat (or try to repeat) that behavior in the future. And positive feedback for effort is an especially effective way to motivate youngsters to work on difficult skills. So rather than shouting and providing negative feedback to a player who has made a mistake, try offering a compliment sandwich, described on page 12.

Sometimes just the way you word feedback can make it more positive than negative. For example, instead of saying, "Don't grip the ball that way," you might say, "Grip the ball this way." Then your players will be focusing on what *to* do instead of what *not* to do.

You can give positive feedback verbally and nonverbally. Telling a player, especially in front of teammates, that she or he has performed well is a great way to increase a kid's confidence. And a pat on the back or a handshake can be a very tangible way of communicating your recognition of a player's performance.

Coaches, be positive!

Only a very small percentage of ACEP-trained coaches' behaviors are negative.

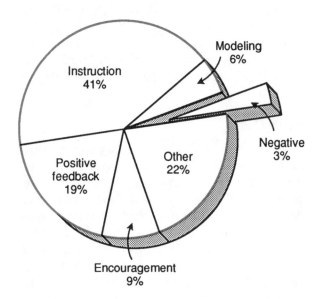

Who Else Do I Need to Communicate With?

Coaching involves not only sending and receiving messages and providing proper feedback to players, but also includes interacting with players' parents, fans, umpires, and opposing coaches. If you don't communicate effectively with these groups of people, your coaching career will be unpleasant and short-lived. So try these suggestions for communicating with each group.

Parents

A player's parents need to be assured that their son or daughter is under the direction of a coach who is both knowledgeable about softball and concerned about the youngster's well-being. You can put their worries to rest by holding a preseason parent orientation meeting in which you describe your background and your approach to coaching.

If parents contact you with a concern during the season, listen to them closely and try to offer positive responses. If you need to communicate with parents, catch them after a practice, give them a phone call, or send a note through the mail. Messages sent to parents through children are too often lost, misinterpreted, or forgotten.

Fans

The stands probably won't be overflowing at your games, but that only means that you'll more easily hear the one or two fans who criticize your coaching. When you hear something negative said about the job you're doing, don't respond. Keep calm, consider whether the message had any value, and if not, forget it. The best approach is to put away your "rabbit ears" and communicate to fans through your actions that you are a confident, competent coach.

Even if you are ready to withstand the negative comments of fans, your players may not be. Prepare them. Tell them that it is you, not the spectators, to whom they should listen. If you notice that one of your players is rattled by a fan's comment, reassure the player that your evaluation is more objective and favorable—and the one that counts.

Umpires

Your style of communication with umpires will have a great influence on the way your players behave toward them. Therefore, you need to set an example. Greet umpires with a handshake, an introduction, and perhaps some casual conversation about the upcoming contest. Indicate your respect for them before, during, and after the game.

Umpires work extremely hard at their jobs, so don't make nasty remarks, shout, or use disrespectful body gestures. Your players will see you do it, and they'll get the idea that such behavior is appropriate. Plus, if the umpire hears or sees you, the communication between the two of you will break down. In short, you take care of the coaching, and let the umpires call the game.

Opposing Coaches

Make an effort to visit with the coach of the opposing team before the game. Perhaps the two of you can work out a special arrangement for the game, such as free substitution or starting batters with a 1-and-1 count to speed up the game. During the game, don't get into a personal feud with the opposing coach. Remember, it's the kids, not the coaches, who are competing.

Summary Checklist

Now, check your coach-communication skills by answering yes or no to the following questions.

	Yes	No
1. Are your verbal messages to your players positive and honest?	____	____
2. Do you speak loudly, clearly, and in a language your athletes understand?	____	____
3. Do you remember to repeat instructions to your players, in case they didn't hear you the first time?	____	____
4. Are the tone of your voice and your nonverbal messages consistent with the words you use?	____	____
5. Do your facial expressions and body language express interest in and happiness with your coaching role?	____	____
6. Are you attentive to your players and able to pick up even their small verbal and nonverbal cues?	____	____

	Yes	No
7. Do you really care about what your athletes say to you?	——	——
8. Do you instruct rather than criticize when your players make errors?	——	——
9. Are you usually positive when responding to things your athletes say and do?	——	——
10. Do you try to communicate in a cooperative and respectful manner with players' parents, fans, umpires, and opposing coaches?	——	——

If you answered "No" to any of these questions, you may want to refer back to the section of the chapter where the topic was discussed. *Now* is the time to address communication problems, not when you're coaching your players.

UNIT 4

How Do I Get My Team Ready to Play?

 To coach softball, you must understand its basic rules, skills, and strategies. Units 6 through 8 of this *Rookie Coaches Softball Guide* provide the basic information you'll need to comprehend the sport.

But all the softball knowledge in the world will do you little good unless you present it effectively to your players. That's why this unit is so important. In it you will learn the steps to take in teaching sport skills, as well as practical guidelines for planning your season and individual practices.

How Do I Teach Sport Skills?

Many people believe that the only qualification needed to coach is to have played the sport. It's helpful to have played, but there is much more to coaching successfully. And even if you haven't played softball, you can still teach the skills of the game effectively using this IDEA:

I—Introduce the skill.

D—Demonstrate the skill.

E—Explain the skill.

A—Attend to players practicing the skill.

Introduce the Skill

Players, especially young and inexperienced players, need to know what skill they are learning and why they are learning it. You should, therefore, take these three steps every time you introduce a skill to your players:

1. Get your players' attention.
2. Name the skill.
3. Explain the importance of the skill.

Get Your Players' Attention

Because youngsters are easily distracted, use some method to get their attention. Some coaches use captivating news items or stories. Others use jokes. And others simply project an enthusiasm that heightens their players' interest. Whatever method you use, speak slightly above the normal volume and look your players in the eye when you speak. Also arrange the players in two or three evenly spaced rows, facing you but not facing the sun or some source of distraction. Then check that all can see and hear you before you begin.

Name the Skill

Although you might mention other common names for the skill, decide which one you'll use and stick with it. This will help avoid confusion and enhance communication among your players. Also, when you use a term with more than one meaning, like "catch" (what you do in the catcher position versus what you do when you receive and hold onto the ball), make certain players know which you mean.

Explain the Importance of the Skill

Although the importance of a skill may be apparent to you, your players may be less able to see how the skill will help them become better softball players. Offer them a reason for learning the skill and describe how the skill relates to more advanced skills.

The most difficult aspect of coaching is this: Coaches must learn to let athletes learn. Sport skills should be taught so they have meaning to the child, not just meaning to the coach.

Rainer Martens, ACEP Founder

Demonstrate the Skill

The demonstration step is the most important part of teaching softball skills to young players who may have never done anything that closely resembles the skill. They need a picture, not just words. They need to *see* how the skill is performed.

If you are unable to perform the skill correctly, have an assistant coach or someone skilled in softball perform the demonstration. These tips will help make your demonstrations more effective:

- Use correct form.
- Demonstrate the skill several times.
- Slow the skill down, if possible, during one or two performances so that players can see every movement involved in the skill.
- Perform the skill at different angles so that your players can get a full perspective of it.
- Demonstrate the skill with both the right and left hand.

Explain the Skill

Players learn more effectively if they're given a brief explanation of the skill along with the demonstration. Use simple terms to describe the skill, and, if possible, relate the skill to previously learned skills. Ask your players if they understand your description. If one of them looks confused, have her or him explain the skill back to you.

Complex skills often are better understood if they are explained in more manageable parts. For instance, if you want to teach your players how to catch a fly ball, you might take the following steps:

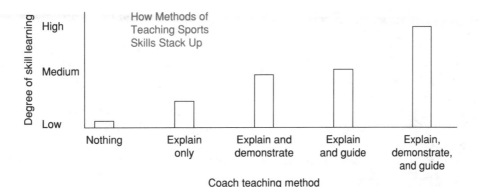

1. Show them a correct performance of the entire skill and explain its function in softball.
2. Break down the skill and point out its component parts to your players.
3. Have players perform each of the component skills you have already taught them, such as being in the ready position when playing the field, getting a good jump on the ball, moving into position to catch it with two hands, and watching the ball all the way into the glove.
4. After players have demonstrated their ability to perform the separate parts of the skill in sequence, reexplain the entire skill.
5. Have them practice the skill.

Attend to Players Practicing the Skill

If the skill you selected was within your players' capabilities and you have done an effective job of introducing, demonstrating, and explaining it, your players should be ready to attempt the skill. Some players may need to be physically guided through the movements during their first few attempts at certain skills. For example, some players may need your hands-on help to grip the ball and position their arms properly on their initial throwing attempts. Walking unsure athletes through the skill in this way will help them gain both confidence and the ability to throw the ball correctly on their own.

Your teaching duties don't end when all your athletes have demonstrated that they understand how to perform the skill. In fact, a significant part of your teaching will involve observing closely the hit-and-miss trial performances of your players.

As you observe players' efforts in drills and activities, offer positive, corrective feedback in the form of the compliment sandwich described in Unit 3. If a player performs the skill properly, acknowledge it and offer praise. Keep in mind that your feedback will have a great influence on your players' motivation to practice and improve their performance.

Remember too that young players need individual instruction. So set aside a time before, during, or after practice to give them individual help.

What Planning Do I Need to Do?

Beginning coaches often make the mistake of showing up for the first practice with no particular plan in mind. These coaches find that their practices are unorganized, that their players are frustrated and inattentive, and that the amount and quality of their skill instruction is limited. Planning is essential to successful teaching *and* coaching. And it doesn't begin on the way to practice!

Preseason Planning

Effective coaches begin planning well before the start of the season. Here are some

preseason steps that will make the season more enjoyable, successful, and safe for you and your players:

- Familiarize yourself with the sport organization you are involved in, especially its philosophy and goals regarding youth sport.
- Examine the availability of facilities, equipment, instructional aids, and other materials needed for practices and games.
- Check to see if you have liability insurance to cover you when one of your players is hurt (see Unit 5). If you don't, get some.
- Establish your coaching priorities regarding having fun, developing players' skills, and winning.
- Select and meet with your assistant coaches to discuss the philosophy, goals, team rules, and plans for the season.
- Register players for the team. Have them complete a player information form and obtain medical clearance forms, if required.
- Institute an injury-prevention program for your players.
- Hold a parent orientation meeting to inform parents of your background, phi-

losophy, goals, and instructional approach. Also, give a brief overview of the league's rules and softball rules, terms, and strategies to familiarize parents or guardians with the sport.

You may be surprised at the number of things you should do even before the first practice. But if you address them during the preseason, the season will be much more enjoyable and productive for you and your players.

In-Season Planning

Your choice of activities during the season should be based on whether they will help your players develop physical and mental skills, knowledge of rules and game tactics, sportsmanship, and love for softball. All of these goals are important, but we'll focus on the skills and tactics of softball to give you an idea of how to itemize your objectives.

Goal Setting

What you plan to do during the season must be reasonable for the maturity and skill level of your players. In terms of softball skills and strategies, you should teach young players the basics and move on to more complex activities only after they have mastered these easier techniques and tactics.

To begin the season, your instructional goals might include the following:

- Players will be able to assume and maintain the ready position.
- Players will be able to throw overhand.
- Players who pitch will be able to use correct technique and throw strikes.
- Players will be able to catch a thrown ball.
- Players will be able to catch a fly ball.
- Players will be able to field a ground ball.
- Players will be able to sacrifice bunt consistently.
- Players will be able to make consistent, fundamentally correct swings and make contact with the ball.
- Players will be able to slide correctly into bases.

- Players will demonstrate knowledge of softball rules.
- Players will demonstrate knowledge of basic concepts of team defense.
- Players will demonstrate knowledge of baserunning fundamentals.

Organizing

After you've defined the skills and tactics you want your players to learn during the season, you can plan how to teach them to your players in practices. But be flexible! If your players are having difficulty learning a skill or tactic, take some extra time until they get the hang of it—even if that means moving back your schedule. After all, if your players are unable to perform the fundamental skills, they'll never execute the more complex skills you have scheduled for them.

Still, it helps to have a plan for progressing players through skills during the season. The sample 8-week season plan in the appendix shows how to schedule your skill instruction in an organized and progressive manner. If this is your first softball coaching experience, you may wish to follow the plan as it stands. If you have some previous experience, you may want to modify the schedule to better fit the needs of your team.

What Makes Up a Good Practice?

A good instructional plan makes practice preparation much easier. Have players work on more important and less difficult goals in early season practice sessions. And see to it that players master basic skills before moving on to more advanced ones.

It is helpful to establish *one objective* for each practice, but try to include a *variety of activities* related to that objective. For example, although your primary objective might be to improve players' hitting skill, you should have players perform several different drills designed to enhance that single skill. And, to interject further variety into your practices, vary the order of the activities you schedule for players to perform.

In general, we recommend that you cover the following in each practice:

- *Warm up*
- *Practice previously taught skills*
- *Teach and practice new skills*
- *Practice under game-like conditions*
- *Cool down*
- *Evaluate*

Warm Up

As you're checking the roster and announcing the performance objectives for the practice, your players should be preparing their bodies for vigorous activity. A 5- to 10-minute period of easy-paced activities (e.g., half-speed running around the bases), stretching (see page 30), and calisthenics should be sufficient for youngsters to limber their muscles and reduce the risk of injury.

Practice Previously Taught Skills

Devote part of each practice to having players work on the fundamental skills they already know. But remember, kids like variety. So organize and modify drills to keep everyone involved and interested. Praise and encourage players when you notice improvement, and offer individual assistance to those who need help.

Teach and Practice New Skills

Gradually build on your players' existing skills by giving them something new to practice each session. The proper method for teaching sport skills is described on pages 19 to 21. Refer to those pages if you have any questions about teaching new skills or if you want to evaluate your teaching approach periodically during the season.

Practice Under Game-Like Conditions

Competition among teammates during practices prepares players for actual games and informs young athletes about their abilities relative to those of their peers. Youngsters also seem to have more fun in competitive activities.

You can create game-like conditions by using competitive drills and practice games (see Units 7 and 8). However, consider the following guidelines before introducing competition into your practices.

- Provide all players an equal opportunity to participate.
- Match players by ability and physical maturity.
- Make certain players can execute fundamental skills before they compete in groups.
- Emphasize performing well, not winning, in every competition.
- Give players room to make mistakes by avoiding constant evaluation of their performances.

Cool Down

Each practice should wind down with a 5- to 10-minute period of light exercise, including jogging, performance of simple skills, and some stretching. The cool-down allows athletes' bodies to return to the resting state and avoid stiffness, and affords you an opportunity to review the practice.

Evaluate

At the end of practice spend a few minutes with your players reviewing how well the session accomplished the objective you had set. Even if your evaluation is negative, show optimism for future practices and send players off on an upbeat note.

How Do I Put a Practice Together?

Simply knowing the six practice components is not enough. You must also be able to arrange those components into a logical progression and fit them into a time schedule. Now, using your instructional goals as a guide for selecting what skills to have your players work on, try to plan several softball practices you might conduct. The following example should help you get started.

Sample Practice Plan

Performance Objective. Players will be able to field ground balls and fly balls and correctly position themselves defensively.

Component	Time	Activity or drill
Warm-up	10 min	Half-speed running around field Calisthenics
Practice previously taught skills	15 min	Throwing Knee drill and Windmill drill (see page 41)
Teach	10 min	Positioning to field balls hit in the air and on the ground
Practice	20 min	Position and catch drill Position and field drill Shift and block drill (catchers)
Practice game	15 min	Modified game—players rotate positions, coach hits to all areas of the field, players run bases
Cool down and evaluate	10 min	Easy throwing Jogging Stretching

Summary Checklist

During your softball season, check your teaching and planning skills periodically. As you gain more coaching experience, you should be able to answer "Yes" to each of the following questions:

When you teach sport skills to your players, do you

_____ arrange the players so all can see and hear?

_____ introduce the skill clearly and explain its importance?

_____ demonstrate the skill properly several times?

_____ explain the skill simply and accurately?

_____ attend closely to players practicing the skill?

_____ offer corrective, positive feedback or praise after observing players' attempts at the skill?

When you plan, do you remember to plan for

_____ preseason events like player registration, liability protection, use of facilities, and parent orientation?

_____ season goals such as the development of players' physical skills, mental skills, sportsmanship, and enjoyment?

_____ practice components such as warm-up, practicing previously taught skills, teaching and practicing new skills, practicing under competitive conditions, cool-down, and evaluation?

UNIT 5

What About Safety?

One of your players rounds third, heading for home. She makes a hard slide into the plate as the catcher tags her. The umpire rules "safe," but you stop cheering when you notice that your player is unable to get on her feet and seems to be in pain. What do you do?

One of the least pleasant aspects of coaching is seeing players get hurt. Fortunately, there are many preventive measures coaches can institute to reduce the risk. But in spite of such efforts, injury remains a reality of sport participation. Consequently, you must be prepared to provide first aid when injuries occur and to protect yourself against unjustified lawsuits. This unit will describe how you can

- create the safest possible environment for your players,
- provide emergency first aid to players when they get hurt, and
- protect yourself from injury liability.

How Do I Keep My Players From Getting Hurt?

Injuries may occur because of poor preventive measures. Part of your planning, described in Unit 4, should include steps that give your players the best possible chance for injury-free participation. These steps include the following:

- *Preseason physical examination*
- *Physical conditioning*
- *Apparel and facilities inspection*
- *Equipment inspection*
- *Matching athletes and warning of inherent risks*
- *Proper supervision and record keeping*
- *Sufficient hydration*
- *Warm-up and cool-down*

Preseason Physical Examination

Even in the absence of severe injury or ongoing illness, your players should have a physical examination every 2 years. If a player has a known complication, a physician's consent should be obtained before participation is allowed. You should also have players' parents or guardians sign a participation agreement form and a release form to allow their child to be treated in the case of an emergency.

Physical Conditioning

Muscles, tendons, and ligaments unaccustomed to vigorous and long-lasting physical activity are prone to injury. Therefore, prepare your athletes to withstand the exertion of playing softball. An effective conditioning program would include running, throwing, and swinging activities.

Make conditioning drills and activities fun. Include a skill component—such as baserunning, throwing hard, or catching fly balls—to prevent players from becoming bored or looking upon the activity as "work."

Apparel and Facilities Inspection

Another means to prevent injuries is to check the quality and fit of the clothes worn by your players. Uncleated, poor-fitting, or unlaced softball shoes, unstrapped eyeglasses, and jewelry are dangerous on the softball field—both to the player wearing such items and to other participants.

Remember to examine regularly the field on which your players practice and play. Remove hazards, report conditions you cannot remedy, and request maintenance as necessary.

Equipment Inspection

You should also inspect all the batting helmets; each should have protective ear flaps.

INFORMED CONSENT FORM

I hereby give my permission for _____ to participate in

_____ during the athletic season beginning in 199___. Further, I authorize the school to provide emergency treatment of an injury to or illness of my child if qualified medical personnel consider treatment necessary *and* perform the treatment. This authorization is granted only if I cannot be reached and a reasonable effort has been made to do so.

Date _____   Parent or guardian _____

Address _____   Phone (____)_____

Family physician _____   Phone (____)_____

Pre-existing medical conditions (e.g., allergies or chronic illnesses) _____

_____

Other(s) to also contact in case of emergency _____

Relationship to child _____   Phone(____)_____

My child and I are aware that participating in _____ is a potentially hazardous activity. I assume all risks associated with participation in this sport, including but not limited to falls, contact with other participants, the effects of the weather, traffic, and other reasonable risk conditions associated with the sport. All such risks to my child are known and understood by me.

I understand this informed consent form and agree to its conditions on behalf of my child.

Child's signature _____   Date_____

Parent's signature _____   Date_____

And to prevent needless "strawberries," encourage your players to wear padded sliding shorts, available through most sporting goods outlets.

Matching Athletes and Warning of Inherent Risks

Children of the same age may differ in height and weight by up to 6 inches and 50 pounds. The bigger child will likely hit and throw the ball much harder and farther than the smaller one. That's why it's important to match players against opponents of similar physical maturity and size, and not simply according to age. Such an approach gives smaller, less mature children a better chance to succeed and avoid injury, and provides larger children with more of a challenge. Experience, ability, and emotional maturity are other important factors to keep in mind in practice and in games.

Matching helps protect you from certain liability concerns. But you also must warn players of the inherent risks involved in playing softball, because "failure to warn" is one of the most successful arguments in lawsuits against coaches. So, thoroughly explain the inherent risks of softball and make sure each player knows, understands, and appreciates those risks.

The preseason parent orientation meeting is a good opportunity to explain the risks of the sport to parents and players. It is also a good occasion to have both the players and their parents sign waivers releasing you from liability were an injury to occur. Such waivers do not discharge you of responsibility for your players' well-being, but they are recommended by lawyers.

Proper Supervision and Record Keeping

With youngsters, your mere presence in the area of play is not enough; you must actively plan and direct team activities and closely observe and evaluate players' participation. You're the watchdog responsible for their welfare. So if you notice a player limping or grimacing, remove him or her from the game and examine the extent of the injury.

As a coach, you're also required to enforce the rules of the sport, prohibit dangerous horseplay, and hold practices only under safe weather conditions. Fulfilling these specific supervisory responsibilities will make the play environment safer for your players and will help protect you from liability should an injury occur.

For further protection, keep records of your season plans, practice plans, and players' injuries. Season and practice plans come in handy when you need evidence that players have been taught certain skills, and accurate, detailed accident report forms offer protection against unfounded lawsuits. Ask for these forms from the organization for whom you coach. And hold on to these records for several years so that an "old softball injury" of a former player doesn't come back to haunt you.

Sufficient Hydration

The hot sun combined with physical activity can take its toll on a young player. The loss of body fluids through sweating can cause cramps, heat exhaustion, or worse. Unfortunately, players are often late in realizing their water deficiency because it occurs long before they're thirsty. So make sure you have a large supply of cool water available for players to drink during and after practice. And periodically remind them to take water breaks between activities.

Warm-Up and Cool-Down

Although young bodies are generally very limber, they too can get tight from inactivity. Therefore, a warm-up period of approximately 10 minutes before each practice is strongly recommended. The warm-up should address each muscle group and get the heart rate elevated in preparation for strenuous activity. Moderate-paced running followed by stretching activities is a common sequence. Some effective stretches for softball include the shoulder, upper body, groin, and leg stretches shown in Figure 5.1, a-d. Be especially certain that players loosen up throwing arms before performing skills or drills that require them to throw the ball.

Tips for Stretching

Here are some guidelines that will enhance your players' flexibility and decrease the likelihood of injury because of tight muscles:

- Stretch only to a point of mild muscle tension during initial stretches, and increase the degree of tension upon subsequent attempts.
- *Never* stretch to the point of pain.
- Hold each stretch for 10 to 15 seconds, counting silently to yourself.
- Breath slowly and steadily; don't hold your breath during a stretch!
- Stretch both sides of the body equally (e.g., if you stretch the right hamstring 5 times, do the same for the left hamstring).

As practice is winding down, slow players' heart rates with an easy jog or walk. Then arrange for a 5- or 10-minute period of easy stretching at the end of practice to help players avoid stiff arm and leg muscles and to make them less tight before the next practice.

What If One of My Players Gets Hurt?

No matter how good and thorough your prevention program, injuries will occur. And when injury does strike, chances are you will be the one in charge. The severity and nature of the injury will determine how actively involved you'll be in treating the in-

Figure 5.1   Stretches for the (a) shoulder, (b) groin, (c) upper body, and (d) legs.

jury. But regardless of how seriously a player is hurt, it is your responsibility to know what steps to take. So let's look at how you can provide *basic* emergency care to your injured athletes.

Minor Injuries

Although no injury seems minor to the person experiencing it, most injuries are neither life-threatening nor severe enough to restrict participation. And when such injuries occur, you can take an active role in their initial treatment.

Scrapes and Cuts

When one of your players has an open wound, follow these three steps:

1. Stop the bleeding by applying direct pressure with a clean dressing to the wound and elevating the wounded area. *Do not* remove the dressing if it becomes blood-soaked. Instead, place an additional dressing on top of the one already in place. If bleeding continues, elevate the injured area above the heart and maintain pressure.

2. Cleanse the wound thoroughly once the bleeding is controlled. A good rinsing with a forceful stream of water, and perhaps light scrubbing with soap, will help prevent infection.

3. Protect the wound with sterile gauze or a bandage. If the player continues to participate, apply protective padding over the injured area.

For bloody noses not associated with serious facial injury, have the athlete sit and lean slightly forward. Then pinch the player's nostrils shut. If the bleeding continues after 10 minutes or if the athlete has a history of nosebleeds, seek medical assistance.

Sprains and Strains

The physical demands of softball practices and games often result in injury to the muscles or tendons (strains) or to the ligaments (sprains). When your players suffer minor strains or sprains, immediately apply the RICE method of injury care (see p. 32).

Bumps and Bruises

Inevitably, softball players make contact with each other, bases, the fence, or the playing field. And if the force at impact is great enough, a bump or bruise will result. Many players will continue playing with such sore spots. But if the bump or bruise is large and painful, you should react appropriately. Enact the RICE formula for injury care and monitor the injury. If swelling, discoloration, and pain have lessened, the player may resume participation with protective padding; if not, the player should be examined by a physician.

Serious Injuries

Head, neck, and back injuries, fractures, and injuries that cause a player to lose consciousness are among a class of injuries that you cannot and *should not try to treat* yourself. But you *should plan* what you'll do if such an injury occurs. And your plan should include the following guidelines for action:

- Obtain the phone number and ensure the availability of nearby emergency care units.
- Assign an assistant coach or another *adult* the responsibility of contacting emergency medical help upon your request.
- *Do not move* the injured athlete.
- Calm the injured athlete and keep others away from him or her as much as possible.
- Evaluate whether the athlete's breathing is stopped or irregular, and, if necessary, clear the airway with your fingers.
- Administer artificial respiration if breathing has stopped.
- Administer cardiopulmonary resuscitation (CPR), or have a trained individual administer CPR, if the athlete's circulation has stopped.
- Remain with the athlete until medical personnel arrive.

How Do I Protect Myself?

When one of your players is injured, naturally your first concern is his or her well-being. Your feelings for children, after all, are

The RICE Method

R—Rest the area to avoid further damage and foster healing.

I—Ice the area to reduce swelling and pain.

C—Compress the area by securing an ice bag in place with an elastic wrap.

E—Elevate the injury above heart level to keep the blood from pooling in the area.

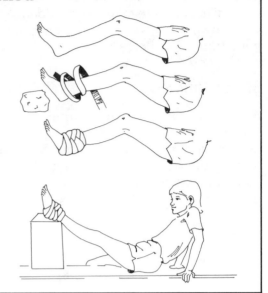

what made you decide to coach. Unfortunately, there is something else that you must consider: Can you be held liable for the injury?

From a legal standpoint, a coach has nine duties to fulfill. We've discussed all but planning (see Unit 4) and equipment (see Unit 6) in this unit.

1. Provide a safe environment.
2. Properly plan the activity.
3. Provide adequate and proper equipment.
4. Match athletes by size, maturity, and skill.

5. Warn of inherent risks in the sport.
6. Supervise the activity closely.
7. Evaluate athletes for injury or incapacity.
8. Know emergency procedures and first aid.
9. Keep adequate records.

In addition to fulfilling these nine legal duties, you should check your insurance coverage to make sure your present policy will protect you from liability.

Summary Self-Test

Now that you've read how to make your coaching experience safe for your players and yourself, test your knowledge of the material by answering these questions:

1. What are eight injury prevention measures you can institute to try to keep your players from getting hurt?
2. What is the three-step emergency care process for cuts?
3. What method of treatment is best for minor sprains and strains?
4. What steps can you take to manage serious injuries?
5. What are the nine legal duties of a coach?

UNIT
6

What Is Softball All About?

oftball has been played for more than a century in the United States. Now it is the #1 participant sport in America, with more than 35 million players and about 1/4 million teams competing each summer at all levels of play, fast and slow pitch. Both versions of the game require quick reactions and a number of offensive and defensive skills. But the reason so many people are playing softball is because it's fun!

So as you read this unit describing some of the basic rules of the game and Units 7 and 8 covering the sport's skills and strategies, don't get bogged down. Keep in mind that along with your duties to protect and instruct, you are also responsible for providing an atmosphere in which your players can fully enjoy participating. And if you do provide that atmosphere, your players will be more likely to continue their softball careers and experience the fun of softball for the rest of their lives.

How Is the Game Played?

The Amateur Softball Association (ASA; see Unit 1) governs the rules of softball. However, your local league may have variations of ASA guidelines. So the first thing to do is to get an up-to-date ASA rule book. Then check with your league's officials to learn of any modifications of the rules stipulated. For example, younger divisions have players hit off a batting tee or pitching machine instead of a pitcher. Also, many youth leagues institute special baserunning and pitching restrictions that are appropriate for particular stages of development.

The remainder of this unit in no way substitutes for the ASA rule book. But it will give you some guidelines to follow and will help you teach your players the rules of the game. We've provided the definitions of common softball terms on page 60. We also encourage you to consult veteran coaches in the league so you—and your players—have no surprises about how the game is conducted.

Softball Is a Hit!

Softball is the fourth most popular sport among high school girls, with more than 200,000 participating each year.

Field of Play

Like baseball, softball is played on a diamond-shaped field. However, you should be aware of the three major differences between the two sports' fields:

- Softball has a dirt infield, whereas baseball is typically played on a grass infield.
- Softball has a flat pitching area, whereas baseball has a pitching mound from which pitchers deliver the ball to the plate.
- Softball has a rather short outfield fence. The distance from the softball fence to home plate is a little more than half the distance from a baseball fence to home plate.

The bases used in softball (sometimes called bags) should be white and square, and they should provide some give upon impact—just as in baseball. Home plate and the pitching rubber are also the same in softball and baseball. Check that both the plate and rubber are in good repair and that the dirt surrounding them is flat, with no big holes dug out that might cause an ankle or knee injury.

Figure 6.1 will give you a better understanding of the softball diamond on which your team will typically play. However, some facilities may not conform exactly to this layout because of space or maintenance limitations. For example, some fields may have a shorter outfield fence in right field than in left field and others may have grass infields. As long as such conditions do not endanger the safety of your ballplayers, there is no reason to be alarmed.

The particular dimensions of the field will differ according to the division of competition. Table 6.1 provides the recommended dimensions for various age groups. The closer the prescribed dimensions to your players' level of development, the more they'll enjoy participating.

Table 6.1   Softball Field Dimensions (Feet) for Four Age Divisions

Age division	Distance between the bases	Distance between pitching rubber and home plate	Distance between home plate and the fence
16 and 15	60	40	200
14 and 13	60	40	175
12 and 11	60	35	175
10 and under	55	35	150

Equipment and Apparel

Softball does not require much equipment, but the equipment your players do use should be of proper specifications and in good repair. The practice and game outfits worn by your players should be comfortable and within the league's rules.

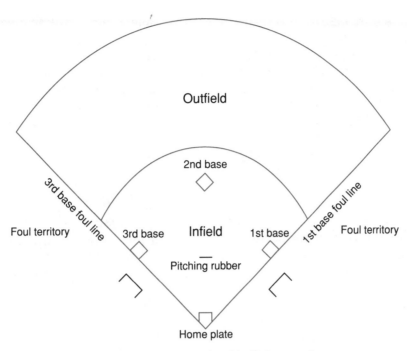

Figure 6.1   Typical softball diamond.

Ball

An 11-inch softball is standard size for most youth leagues. Your league administrators have probably selected the type and brand of ball that is to be used in every game. Try to obtain similar softballs for your practices so that players can get the feel for the seams, texture, and weight of the ball they'll be throwing and hitting in competition.

Bat

Aluminum bats are now far more popular among softball players than wood bats. Both types have a barrel, handle, and knob (see Figure 6.2), but the aluminum bat is lighter and wears better than wood. However, because they last longer and have become *the* bat to use, aluminum bats are more expensive than the wood variety.

Knob   Handle   Barrel

Figure 6.2   Softball bat.

Whatever type of bat a player uses, make sure that it is neither too long nor too heavy. The best way to determine the appropriate-ness of a bat's dimensions is to observe the player swinging it; if it's too big or heavy, it will prevent a smooth swing pattern. Another way to match a player with the correct bat is to have the player swing bats of varying sizes and decide which bat feels most comfortable.

Glove

Every player on the team needs a glove to catch the ball when out in the field. Catchers and first basemen use mitts specially designed for those positions; other infielders use smaller gloves so that they can get the ball out quickly with the throwing hand. Outfielders prefer large, long-fingered gloves that serve as a ''basket'' to catch fly balls.

Whatever gloves your players use, make sure that the size is appropriate and that the pocket is large and flexible enough for the ball to be squeezed when it enters. Also, encourage players to maintain a good pocket by oiling the glove before the season and wrapping a ball in the pocket between practices.

Uniforms

Players' practice and game attire should be comfortable and protective. Loose but not baggy-fitting clothes are best for hitting, running, sliding, catching, and throwing. Also, if your team plays during the heat of summer, recommend that players wear light-colored and lightweight fabrics.

All players should wear baseball or softball shoes with rubber cleats. The shoes should fit properly, and players should double-tie their laces to prevent them from coming untied, which can cause a player to trip.

Batters and base runners should wear helmets at all times to protect their heads. Players in the field should either wear caps or have their hair gathered to keep it out of their eyes. A cap also helps block the sun.

A catcher must be outfitted with a mask, helmet, chest protector, and shin guards before getting behind the plate. Make sure that this protective equipment fits the catcher properly, that it is in good repair, and that the catcher knows how to put it on correctly.

Game Procedures

Softball is played in much the same way as baseball. If you are at all familiar with that sport, you should have no trouble learning the game. If you know little about either sport, here are some basic elements of softball as a foundation before you study the ASA rule book:

- A coin flip is often used to determine who is the home team (and thus bats second).

- In fast pitch, both teams must have nine players participating in the game at any one time. In addition, each team may have one designated hitter, who may substitute at bat for any player in the field. In slow pitch a tenth position, short fielder, is added to both team's roster.

- Pitchers must throw the ball underhand, with a very small arc in fast pitch, and a 6 to 12 foot arc in slow pitch (see Figure 6.3).

- Each batter is allowed a maximum of 3 strikes or 4 balls. Many slow pitch leagues start each batter at a 1-1 count.

- A batter makes an out by striking out (3 strikes), grounding out (the ball touches the ground before being caught and is thrown to first base before the batter arrives), or flying out (the ball is caught by a fielder before it touches the ground).

- A batter gets on base by getting a walk (4 balls or hit by a pitch), getting a hit (hitting the ball where the defense cannot catch it or cannot relay it to first base before the batter arrives), or because of an error by the defense.

- A base runner cannot leave a base until the pitcher releases the ball.

- The offensive team hits until it makes 3 outs.

- An inning is completed when both teams have made 3 outs.

- A run is scored if an offensive player

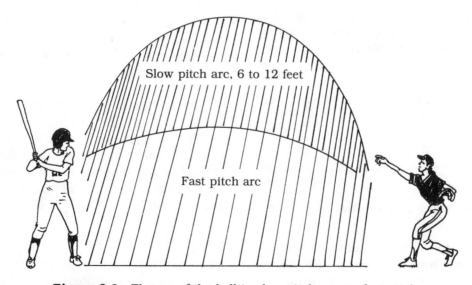

Figure 6.3   The arc of the ball in slow pitch versus fast pitch.

reaches first, second, and third bases and home plate without being tagged out or forced out (the defensive team touches the base to which the player is going before the player arrives; the player has no alternative but to try for the base because a teammate is on the base behind).

- A game consists of 7 innings; if after 7 innings the score is tied, additional innings are played until the tie is broken at the conclusion of an inning.
- The team with the most runs at the end of the game wins.

Umpires

The rules of softball are enforced on the field by officials called umpires. Before the game, the umpires will hold a meeting with both coaches, who exchange their lineups. The umpires will note any unusual rules or special warnings at that time.

Ideally, an umpire is assigned to both outfield foul lines, each base, and home plate. However, youth leagues rarely have more than two umpires—one at home plate and another between first and second base.

The home plate umpire is the ultimate decision-maker on any ruling. The home

plate umpire also calls balls and strikes on all pitches that are not hit into play. The "strike zone" is an area defined vertically from the top of the batter's knees up to the armpit area and horizontally by the width of the plate (see Figure 6.4).

Base umpires rule on such things as whether a fielder caught a ball before it touched the ground and whether a base runner beat a throw to the base. If a ball and a runner arrive at the same time at a base, the runner is ruled safe.

Player Positions

Now that you have a general understanding of the rules, you need to consider how to best prepare your team to play within those guidelines. One of your most difficult decisions will be positioning players in the field and setting the lineup in a way that accentuates their strengths and falls within their interests.

Try to give your players experience at a variety of positions throughout the season. It will expand their skills and understanding of the game, and some of your players may exhibit skills at one position that they would have never demonstrated at another defensive spot. Following is a listing, a brief description, and an illustration (see Figure 6.5) of each softball position, with the number assigned to the position given in parentheses.

Pitcher (1)—This player will be a good athlete and a tough and smart competitor. She or he must have a very good arm, be able to throw strikes consistently, and maintain her or his poise throughout the game.

Catcher (2)—The player you position behind the plate must be tough and sturdy to withstand the rigors of catching. Great hand-eye coordination is necessary for receiving pitches, and a strong and accurate throwing arm is required for getting the ball to any of the bases.

First baseman (3)—The first baseman should be tall to provide a big target for infielders and be able to stretch out from the base to receive throws. Superior catching ability is essential to this position.

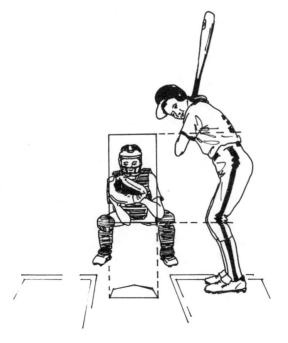

Figure 6.4   The strike zone.

Second baseman (4)—To play second base effectively, a player needs lateral quickness and sound fielding fundamentals.

Third baseman (5)—The player who fields ground balls the best and can both charge bunts and react quickly to snag line shots is the one you want in the "hot corner."

Shortstop (6)—A very good athlete with excellent agility and a strong throwing arm should fill the shortstop position.

Left fielder (7)—Fill this position with a player who is very good at catching pop flies.

Center fielder (8)—Speed and smarts are required to cover the large area in center field and to position correctly for each hitter.

Right fielder (9)—Catching fly balls and throwing strongly to the cutoff person or base are two skills required for the right field position.

Short fielder (10)—Used only in slow pitch.

This player should be fast and sure-handed and be an accurate thrower to get to, catch, and relay balls hit past the infielders.

Designated hitter (DH)—The DH may bat for any player in the field; therefore, this player should be one of your best hitters who perhaps has some fielding deficiencies.

Coaches' Roles

Now that you have the rules down and the team organized, what do you and your assistants do during the game? When your team is batting, third and first base coaching boxes are provided for you to give signals to hitters and direct runners on the base paths. When your team is in the field, stay involved by positioning players for each hitter, closely observing the performance of your pitcher, and encouraging everyone—in the field and on the bench—to keep focused on the game.

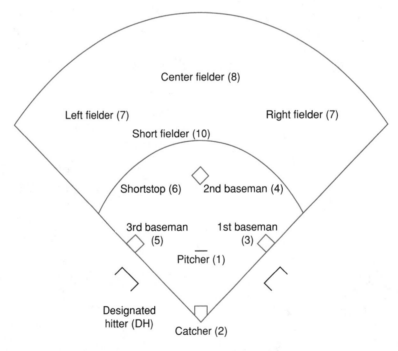

Figure 6.5 Player positions in softball.

UNIT 7

What Softball Skills and Drills Should I Teach?

Coaching softball can sometimes seem overwhelming because each position involves so many skills. The important thing is to avoid trying to teach everything. Softball skills can be broken down into four categories:

- *Throwing*
- *Catching*
- *Baserunning*
- *Hitting*

When you are working with young athletes, you have to decide how detailed your instruction will be. Emphasize the basics so that young players have a solid foundation on which to build. Break down the skills as much as possible, but present information or have players work on each of the four skills in every practice. For instance, when teaching throwing you would start with the overhand throw, but you might not talk about the snap throw until you feel your players are ready for a new skill. With very young players be creative—make drills short and fun. Use a yarn ball or a rubber or small-size softball, if necessary, to eliminate fear. Remember, always practice form before action.

Information on how to conduct practice is discussed later, but obviously time plays a big role in how much information you can teach to your team. We'll give you some tips in this unit and in Unit 8 on how to maximize your instruction in the limited practice time you do have.

The following information will help you teach players the basics.

Throwing

Throwing is one of those so-called boring skills that athletes hate to work on. Not surprisingly, therefore, you will find that the ability to throw the ball is one of the weakest skills of all your players. Very often, even those athletes with strong arms have poor fundamentals. So set aside time in the beginning of every practice to work on throws, and monitor players during this warm-up. Make sure they are performing the skill the way you are teaching it; don't let them develop bad throwing habits.

Overhand Throw

When teaching this skill, don't just let your players partner up and throw the ball back and forth. Start them in a progression and have them repeat these steps until the overhand throw becomes natural to them. Even older athletes tend to cut corners when throwing, so pay close attention to each step.

1. A player faces a target, with a ball in the throwing hand. Then the player steps forward with the ball-side leg to begin momentum forward.
2. The player brings the glove-side foot forward while rotating the shoulders and hips back and pushing the weight back on the ball-side foot (see Figure

7.1). At this point the player's glove-side shoulder should be pointed toward the target, his or her throwing arm extended back, and the wrist cocked.

Figure 7.1   The start of the overhand throw.

3. As the throw is made, the player should shift weight to the front foot, and the player's arm should be brought up with the elbow passing by the head, just above the ball-side ear (see Figure 7.2).

Figure 7.2   Midpoint in the overhand throw.

4. The shoulders rotate back, square to the target, allowing the throwing arm to come through with the hand extended down by the glove-side knee (see Figure 7.3).

Figure 7.3 Follow-through of the overhand throw.

Encourage your players to snap down on the throw with maximum acceleration. Also, remind them that the farther the distance of the throw, the higher they must release the ball in their throwing motion.

Throwing Drills

Name. **Knee Drill**

Purpose. To isolate the upper body in the throwing motion

Organization. Start one line of players down the foul line and line up their partners opposite them 15 to 20 feet apart. Players drop down on one knee with the glove-side leg forward. They then rotate the trunk, point the glove-side shoulder to the target, bring the throwing arm back, cock the wrist, and follow through after releasing the ball (see Figure 7.4).

Figure 7.4 Knee drill.

Coaching Points. Have your players stand to receive the throw if they have problems catching the ball while down on one knee.

Name. **Windmill Drill**

Purpose. To emphasize getting full arm extension on every throw

Organization. Position players approximately the same distance apart as in the Knee Drill. From an upright position, players start a windmill action with the throwing arm, keeping it fully extended. Each player brings her or his arm by the ball-side ear, keeping the weight back until the ball is spiked into the ground in front of the thrower. The player should bend over at the waist with the follow-through.

Coaching Points. Make sure that the players show good arm speed and a strong snap. Watch out for one of the most common errors players make—dropping the elbow of the throwing arm and therefore failing to get full extension during the delivery.

Name. **Target Drill**

Purpose. To help players learn the proper ball release point for throws of various distances and thereby increase their throwing accuracy

Organization. Players stand about 15 feet from the backstop. With a tape, mark a series of targets on the backstop, starting about waist high and moving up to about 20 feet. Executing the proper fundamentals, the players practice their release point by trying to hit a particular target from 15, 25, 45, and 60 feet.

Coaching Points. Make sure the players get full arm extension, and don't let them drop their elbows. Players who cannot throw long distances without using improper mechanics should remain near the target.

Snap Throw

The snap throw is often overlooked by coaches, but it is one of the most important throws in softball. It is used to get the ball quickly and accurately to another player a short distance away without overpowering him or her. Like the overhand throw, it can be taught in a simple progression and once learned can eliminate a lot of throwing errors.

1. Facing a partner, the player brings the ball up to the ear with the arm bent.
2. The player extends the throwing arm toward the person receiving the ball, aiming to hit the player in the chest.
3. The thrower's arm should be parallel to the ground after the follow-through, with the hand and the finger pointed toward the target (see Figure 7.5).

Make sure that the hand and the arm go straight toward the partner. If the player brings the throwing arm across the body or follows through past a point parallel to the ground, the ball will go wide of the target or too low. At higher levels, this is the throw used in rundowns, so it is important that players learn from the beginning to be accurate with their throws.

Figure 7.5 In the snap throw, the arm ends parallel to the ground.

Error Detection and Correction for Snap Throws

In the excitement of the game, short throws are often overthrown, so players should work hard on mastering the snap throw.

ERROR

Player makes poor short throws, either too low or off to one side.

Figure 7.6 When initiating the snap throw, bring the arm up so that it's perpendicular to the ground.

CORRECTION

1. Remind the thrower to stop the throwing arm at the point perpendicular to the ground when initiating the delivery (see Figure 7.6).
2. On the follow-through, the player must throw directly at the target and not across the body.

Crow Hop

Because of the distances involved in most throws from the outfield, an outfielder needs to learn a crow hop, a move that uses the body to provide additional power in the throw. You will find that many young players throw strictly with the arm, which greatly restricts how far they can throw and leads to arm injuries. The fundamentals are basically the same as for the overhand throw except the hop allows the outfielder to quickly shift the weight back and gather momentum in order to use the body as well as the arm in the throw.

Crow Hop Fundamentals

1. As the fielder catches the ball, he or she steps forward with the ball-side leg.
2. The player skips on the ball-side foot, rotating the shoulders so that the glove-side shoulder is now pointed toward the target. Maintaining weight on the back leg, the player extends the throwing arm back.
3. The player executes the throw, shifting the weight forward to the front foot. The player's shoulders rotate back square to the target, allowing the throwing arm to come through with the throwing hand ending down by the glove-side knee. The back leg should always step toward the target.

When teaching the crow hop to young players, emphasize certain parts of the skill. To help the players attain maximum height on their throws, have them do a forward roll after a strong follow-through. Again, watch for appropriate arm speed and explosion on their throws.

Pitching

In baseball, the pitcher uses an overhand throwing motion. In softball, the pitcher uses an underhand motion to throw the ball. In fast pitch, speed, movement, and location are the keys to pitching success. In slow pitch, arc and location are most important.

Only a few of your players will be able to pitch with any speed and accuracy. This is a unique skill, which sets apart the pitcher from the rest of the team. In fast pitch, a team's success is often determined by the performance of its pitcher, so that one position deserves considerable attention.

Fast pitching is a *very specialized skill*, requiring very specialized instruction. If you are a beginning coach, find an experienced pitching coach to work with the pitchers on your team. Also, read books on pitching and attend clinics to become a better coach for your pitchers.

Slow pitching, although not as mechanically complex, requires excellent control. Nothing is worse than playing the field or watching when a slow-pitch pitcher can't find the plate. So you must work with your pitchers to develop their accuracy.

Every league has special rules about pitchers, including whether one or both feet must be on the pitching rubber at the start of the delivery. There also are some general rules that you need to convey to a beginning pitcher.

Fast Pitching Fundamentals

1. The ball is held with the fingers, not in the hand.
2. The grip should be firm but not tight; either a two- or three-finger grip can be used.
3. The premotion is a natural start to prepare for the pitching delivery. It is a controlled motion, and the body does not start the delivery or go forward until this motion is completed.
4. The arm acts like a whip and should be relaxed throughout the motion.
5. A pitcher needs maximum acceleration on the downward swing with complete arm extension for leverage and rotation in a smooth plane parallel to the body.
6. The stride of the glove-side foot should be thought of as a step, not

a lunge or a falling action. It is a controlled movement.

7. The step should be straight toward home plate with the foot landing at no more than a 45° angle to home.

8. The stride should be long enough to maintain the pitcher's balance and to allow for sufficient weight transfer.

9. The weight must be kept back until that explosive moment when the ball is snapped and all the power resources are thrust forward.

Figure 7.7 The pitcher's balance point.

Maintaining Balance

One of the most crucial points in the fast-pitch delivery is the balance point. That is where the throwing hand is at its highest point above the head and the glove-side foot is at its highest point above the ground (see Figure 7.7). This is a critical point in the delivery. Failure to keep the weight back means the weight is shifted forward too soon, forcing the young pitcher to throw with just the arm. Trying to generate power or speed too early in the delivery often leads to this problem. The signs of transferring weight too early are overstriding, putting weight on the front foot only, and moving the head and shoulders forward ahead of the hips and hand.

Shoulder Position

Young pitchers often err by pitching with the shoulder instead of the wrist, leading the action forward with the throwing-arm shoulder as the arm begins the downward swing from the balance point. The *hand* with the ball should always lead the action.

Wrist/Hand Position

A strong wrist snap is crucial for creating speed and movement on the ball. The

---

Error Detection and Correction for the Balance Point

Pitchers often get excited and try to generate speed too early in the delivery. They should work on starting slowly, building speed, and then finishing as fast as they can.

ERROR	CORRECTION
No matter how she or he tries, the pitcher just can't get any speed on the ball, even though she or he has a strong arm.	1. Have the pitcher start the delivery and then stop at the balance point.
	2. The weight should remain back.
	3. Check the pitcher's stride to make sure it is not too long (the glove-side leg should be just slightly ahead of the pitcher's body at the release point).

pitcher must cock the wrist on the downward swing and then snap it at the power point by the hip, as in Figure 7.8. With the fast ball, the palm and the middle finger point directly at home plate; the first and second fingers are the last to come off the ball.

Figure 7.8   The wrist snap in pitching.

Hip Position

The hips, which act as a coil, first store power and then release it just as the hand hits the power point. A common error is for the pitcher to close the hips toward home before the hand reaches the power point, forcing the hand to go around the hip, losing power and direction. This often makes a pitcher spin around the hip, instead of driving down and through directly toward home plate. Remind your pitchers that they cannot pitch through the hip, so they must let the ball beat their hip to the release point. After delivering the pitch, your pitcher needs to bring the ball-side leg toward the plate and assume a fielding position in case the ball is hit back at her or him.

As you can tell, there are many key elements of the pitcher's delivery, from the start of the premotion until the ball is snapped at the power point. That is why you should use drills to break down each component of the delivery so that your pitchers and you can concentrate on one aspect of the skill.

When you are first working with pitchers,

it is helpful to take a sequence of photos or film that can be shown frame by frame. These reproductions will allow you to note fine details and make appropriate corrections. It always helps players to actually see their mistakes.

Pitching Drills

Name.   **Stand and Snap**

Purpose.   To isolate and develop the wrist snap, a key component of pitching motion

Organization.   The pitcher takes a ball or bucket of balls and practices short snaps either into a fence, into the air, or with a partner.

Coaching Points.   It will be helpful, at first, for a partner (probably the catcher) to hold the pitcher's forearm to prevent "elbow snap." Have your young pitchers practice a wrist snap in as many creative ways as possible. Make sure the pitcher is using just the wrist and not the arm or elbow.

Name.   **Progression Drill**

Purpose.   To break down the various skills in pitching so that you can isolate training on each

Organization.   The pitcher stands about 10 feet from a wall with the glove-side shoulder pointed toward an imaginary target. The pitcher brings the throwing arm straight back and then forward to practice the wrist snap only. In other words, the pitcher will not bring the ball up over the head in this drill. After 10 pitches, have the pitcher add a weight shift to the motion.

Coaching Points.   Once you've built a solid foundation, start with the pitcher facing the target and then move through the progression. As the pitcher proceeds through each stage, stop at any point you detect a weakness.

Name.   **Walking**

Purpose.   To teach young pitchers that the pitching motion should be comfortable and natural, just like walking

Organization. When the overall delivery is sound, have the pitcher walk into the pitch, pitch the ball, and then continue walking, shifting weight under control and keeping the body stable. The pitcher should start about 60 feet from the catcher and walk forward. About 40 feet from the catcher, the pitcher plants the right foot and goes into the pitching delivery. After throwing, the pitcher continues to walk toward the catcher a few more steps.

Coaching Points. If the pitcher's motion seems awkward and off balance, he or she probably is throwing his or her weight around unnecessarily.

Slow Pitching Fundamentals

The mechanics of delivering a slow pitch are much the same as those described for fast pitch. However, you should note these important differences:

1. The throwing arm motion is not whip-like, but rather an easy, half-circle movement (see Figure 7.9).
2. The weight transfer to the front foot is gradual, not explosive.
3. The ball is released in front of the body and tossed upward, unlike hip-released bullets in fast pitch.
4. The wrist helps in the throwing mo-

tion, but it is not snapped quickly as it is in fast pitch.
5. Immediately after the follow through, the pitcher takes several steps back for protection and for fielding purposes.

Catching

The second basic skill of softball is catching the ball. This includes catching a thrown ball or catching a fly ball or ground ball hit off a bat. If you can resolve your players' throwing and catching problems, you will eliminate a great many errors that they might commit.

Receiving a Throw

A fielder may receive a throw when covering or not covering a base. Many of the same principles apply in either case.

When accepting a throw at the bag, an infielder needs to sprint to the bag and get in position to receive the ball in the middle of her or his body. Make sure the player faces the target, bends the knees, and has his or her legs slightly more than shoulder-width apart for a good base of support (see Figure 7.10).

Figure 7.9 The half-circle throwing motion in slow pitch pitching.

Figure 7.10 Proper position in preparing to catch the ball.

Then, as when catching a thrown ball anywhere, the player should fully extend the glove arm, keep the head still, and watch the ball into his or her glove. The player should give with the ball as it enters his or her glove.

You also will want to emphasize to players the following catching fundamentals:

- Catch the ball with two hands.
- Keep the glove wide open to accept the ball.
- Do not stand tall; make sure you drop your hips.
- If it is a tag play, don't keep your foot

on the bag, but get in a position to make the tag.
- If it is a force-out, keep your foot on the side of the bag and never on top, where you could get injured.

Catching Throws to First Base

The first baseman needs to be proficient at catching the thrown ball. Not only must she or he receive the throw, but she or he must also keep a foot on the base to get the force-out. Every team needs a solid first baseman, and that player should be drilled every day in the proper way to receive throws.

When the ball is hit on the ground, she or he must retreat to the bag. With the shoulders square to the throw, the player touches the bag with the throwing-arm-side heel and bends the knees. As the throw is made, the first baseman must decide whether she or he needs to catch it in the air, catch it off the ground, or drop to the ground and block it. If the ball can be caught, the fielder must wait until the last possible second, plant a foot on the inside of the bag, and then stretch to meet the ball (see Figure 7.11). After the stretch, the first baseman comes off the bag and into position to throw.

Error Detection and Correction for Catching Balls at First Base

When a first baseman stretches out too soon, he or she makes it difficult or even impossible to catch throws that are not perfect. Stand behind your players when they practice receiving throws, and make sure they are not anticipating good throws.

ERROR	CORRECTION
Player has trouble catching high, but not bad, throws.	1. Stand behind the first baseman and encourage him or her to wait longer before stretching out.
	2. Have a coach throw the ball high to first base repeatedly, within an arm's length overhead.
	3. On high throws the player should bend the knees and shift the weight off the heels in case he or she needs to jump for the ball. As the throw approaches, he or she then extends upward for the catch.

Figure 7.11   First baseman stretching to catch the ball.

Catching Pitchers

The player who catches the most balls is appropriately called the catcher. This is one of the most physically demanding positions in softball—especially in fast pitch. Not only does the catcher have to crouch and provide a glove target behind the plate, but once the ball is thrown the catcher must react quickly to catch it with the glove or block it with the body. The catcher must also think about the count on the batter, the positioning of teammates, and the baserunning strategy of the opposition. So, when you select a catcher, choose a strong, smart, and tough athlete.

Basic Position

The catcher sits up as close to home plate as possible without interfering with the batter's swing. The catcher's position behind the plate is determined by the position of the batter in the batter's box.

The catcher squats down behind home plate with the weight on the balls of the feet. The glove hand should be extended away from the body, thereby showing the pitcher an open glove and a large target. To further increase the size of the target, teach your catchers to align the glove in the center of the body (see Figure 7.12). Also, have them protect the free hand from tipped balls by placing it behind the back or legs.

When a ball is pitched in the dirt, the catcher should try to block the ball and keep it in front of the body. For example, when a ball is thrown in the dirt to the catcher's

Figure 7.12   Basic catcher's position.

right, she or he steps out with the right leg, keeping the ball in the center of the body. The catcher then drags the left leg behind while the glove moves between the legs, as shown in Figure 7.13. The same movements apply on pitches thrown in the dirt to the left side.

When a pitch is thrown in the dirt just in

Figure 7.13   Catcher blocking a ball thrown in the dirt to her right.

front of the catcher, she or he should drop both knees to the ground and slide into the ball. With the back side of the glove on the ground, the catcher places the glove between the legs to execute the block (see Figure 7.14). The catcher should bow the back and bring the chin down to the chest to protect the throat area and to help keep the eyes on the ball.

Figure 7.14 Catcher receiving a pitch thrown in the dirt in front of her.

Throwing Out Base Runners

When runners are on base, your catcher should use the *up* position so that he or she can shift and execute a throw quickly. For this the catcher is positioned with the feet shoulder-width apart and the left foot slightly in front of the right. The glove hand should be extended away from the body, providing a large target. The back should remain parallel to the ground, as shown in Figure 7.15.

When a runner attempts a steal, the catcher should lean into the ball just before catching it. As he or she catches the ball, the catcher should quickly move the glove-side leg forward into throwing position (jump

Figure 7.15 Catcher in the *up* position.

turn), rotate the shoulders parallel to the batter's box, and bring the glove hand to the ear, where it should meet the throwing hand. The catcher can execute the throw by transferring weight from the back leg to the front leg, rotating the shoulders, and following through. The throwing hand should come to the knee while the back leg steps toward second base.

Drills for Catchers

Name. **Shift and Block**

Purpose. To teach the young catcher how to properly react to wild pitches

Organization. Have your catcher put on all his or her equipment and practice this drill in a grassy area. First, tell the catcher to shift and block while holding a ball. Once he or she learns the fundamentals, start tossing balls that he or she can block. Use a yarn or rubber ball to eliminate fear.

Coaching Points. Make sure the catcher prevents the ball from getting past him or her by using the body and glove to completely block the ball. Also, make sure the catcher brings the head down to watch the ball into the glove.

Name. **Jump Turn**

Purpose. To teach the catcher how to move from an up position to a throwing position

Organization. Start the catcher in an up position and then have a coach throw balls to her or him. The catcher should react to the pitch and practice the footwork needed to make a quick throw to second base. Once the catcher has that down, have her or him actually throw the ball to second base.

Coaching Points. The catcher needs to learn to be quick and explosive. A quick release can be just as effective as a strong arm.

Name. **Bunts, Pop-Ups, and Passed Balls**

Purpose. To improve the catcher's ability to react quickly and correctly to a number of situations

Organization. A coach stands in the batter's box with a ball, a catcher is positioned behind the plate, and a pitcher is on the mound with a ball. After the pitcher delivers a pitch to the catcher, the coach creates a situation with the extra ball, either tossing it up in the air for a pop-up, tossing it back to the fence for a wild pitch, or dropping it in front for a bunt. The catcher drops the pitched ball, moves quickly to the ball thrown by the coach, and fires the ball to the pitcher. The catcher repositions, and the coach picks up the ball at the plate.

Coaching Points. Use this drill to have catchers practice several important skills and also to improve their conditioning.

Catching a Fly Ball

Now that you know how to teach the fundamentals of catching thrown balls, let's look at how you can instruct players to catch balls that have been hit. We'll begin with describing how you can teach players to catch balls hit into the air. Both infielders and outfielders need to know the basics of catching a fly ball; both must do so in a game. But this section will primarily talk about outfield fundamentals.

Because infielders stand so close to the hitter, it seems easier to convince them that they must be in a ready position and prepared for action. Outfielders must be in a similarly alert stance. It's your job to convince young outfielders that they must be ready at all times and must maintain the proper ready position (see Figure 7.16). Players should stand with their knees slightly bent, their feet squared and facing home plate, their weight on the balls of their feet, and gloves waist-high.

Figure 7.16 The ready position.

Judging the Ball

Warn outfielders against taking a step forward or backward the instant the ball is hit. Instead, teach your players to hold their position for a count until they know whether the ball is in front of them or over their head. A step in the wrong direction wastes much more time than taking a split second to locate the ball and make the right decision. This is not a hard habit to break; it just takes practice.

Positioning for the Catch

A difficult skill to teach players is to run to the ball at full speed. Most young athletes tend to drift to the ball, which means they time it to arrive at a point just as the ball does, instead of trying to get there early.

Breaking this habit requires spending hours repeating this drill: Toss easy high fly

---

Error Detection and Correction for Anticipating Hits

Outfielders often try to anticipate where a fly ball will be hit by standing with one foot slightly back, ready to take off in a given direction. If they guess wrong, they may misplay the ball.

ERROR	CORRECTION
Outfielder standing with one foot back ends up in an awkward position when the ball goes in another direction.	1. Make sure the fielder is square to the plate when in the ready position. 2. Teach your players to react to the ball instead of trying to guess where it will go.

balls a short distance from the player; encourage the player to run full speed to where he or she thinks the ball will come down and to try to catch it in a proper position. Explain that doing this makes it easier to catch the ball. For example, if the wind is blowing, the player is able to react from the ready position when the wind changes its flight, rather than overrunning or coming up short on the ball.

Once a fielder has run to a fly ball, he or she must approach and catch the ball properly. These tips should help you teach players how:

- Maintain eye contact with the ball at all times.
- Whenever possible, position yourself behind the ball.
- Run with the glove down, in a typical sprinting position.
- Keep the hands down until in position to make the catch.
- Catch the ball in front of the head, with the arms almost fully extended (see Figure 7.17).
- As the catch is made, give with the impact by bringing the glove down and in toward the chest.
- Always get back as fast as possible on a ball hit over your head.

Figure 7.17　Basic position for catching a fly ball.

Drills for Outfielders

Name.　**Position and Catch**

Purpose.　To teach proper fielding position through repetition

Organization.　The fielder starts from a ready position. On command the fielder pretends to be fielding a ball by reaching up. After you are satisfied that the player understands the basics, start tossing the ball to her or him. Then move on to hitting fly balls off a bat to the player.

Coaching Points.　Confidence is very important in catching fly balls. To build this confidence, players first need good fundamentals; then they must repeat the task until they are sure that they can do it. Use a rubber ball if fear is a factor.

Name.　**Shoulder Toss**

Purpose.　To teach young fielders the proper footwork for moving to catch a ball overhead

Organization.　A player stands about 20 feet from you. Tell the player over which of his or her shoulders you will toss the ball. Then throw the ball high enough that the player has time to drop-step back and catch it easily. The drop step simply involves swinging the ball-side leg back and pivoting on the opposite foot to move in the direction of the ball. As the player improves, quit telling him or her where you will toss the ball and make the balls tougher to catch.

Coaching Points.　Don't worry about the positioning of the players' gloves and hands. Proper footwork leads to easy catches. So make sure they know how to drop-step and move their feet quickly to get in the best position to make the catch.

Name.　**Blind Toss**

Purpose.　To teach players to react to a hit, instead of anticipating one

Organization.　A player stands about 20 feet away from you with her or his back to you. When you yell "ball," toss a ball high into the air. The player should turn around, locate the ball, and catch it.

Coaching Points. This is a confidence builder. It teaches players that they can get to a ball much quicker than they think they can.

Catching a Ground Ball

Along with fly balls, both infielders and outfielders will have to know how to field ground balls. When a ball is hit on the ground to an infielder, the player must position his or her body in front of the ball. Teach your players to always lead with the glove, no matter which direction they move. For a ball hit directly at him or her, the player should move toward the ball under control, charging only on the slow roller. With your instruction and a lot of practice, the player will be able to "pick his or her hop," or anticipate where the last bounce of the ball and predict the best place to catch the ball after it takes that bounce. The player should then move in to field the ball at that point (see Figure 7.18).

Figure 7.18 Softball player "picking his hop."

Teach your players never to back up on a ground ball or a one-hop line drive. If the ball hits about 7 feet from the player or closer, the player must charge and block, keeping the head down and watching the ball all the way into the glove. Even if the ball is not fielded cleanly, there is plenty of time to pick it up and throw the runner out. To eliminate fear, you might want to use safety balls.

Here are some other tips on fielding a ground ball:

- Arms should be extended in front of the body to reach out for the ball.
- On balls with little hop, place the back of the glove, not just the tip, on the ground.
- Watch the ball all the way into the glove.
- Give with the force of the ball for "soft" hands.
- When fielding the ball, take a small hop to make the legs more than shoulder-width apart, and bend the knees slightly.
- If a ball is dropped, always pick it up bare-handed, not with the glove.

Outfielders should catch most ground balls just like an infielder. However, in the outfield, if there is any chance that the ball might get by a player, she or he should drop down on one knee and use the other leg and the body to block the ball. So teach your outfielder to get down early and stay in front of balls that are difficult to field.

Drills for Infielders

Name. **Position and Field**

Purpose. To give young infielders a proper foundation for fielding a ground ball

Organization. Players start in the ready position; on command, they drop down to a fielding position. They will have to incorporate a step and hop in order to drop down. When they have mastered this skill, add a ball, and roll a grounder to one of the players. Every player should respond as if the ball was hit to her or him.

Coaching Points. Make certain that players' switches from the ready to the fielding position are smooth and quick. Don't let them be too mechanical.

Name. **Partner Toss**

Purpose. To eliminate players' fear of the ball to allow them time to get in proper position on grounders

Organization. Partners stand about 20 feet

apart and roll slow ground balls back and forth, emphasizing proper fielding fundamentals. Players should work on getting down, reaching out, and giving with the ball.

Coaching Points.   At first, don't let players use their gloves. Then, after several successful catches apiece, have players put on their gloves. This will help teach them to catch with two hands and get down.

Name.   **Wall Drill**

Purpose.   To practice fielding fundamentals and game reactions in situations where players can't predict the bounce of the ball

Organization.   A group of infielders stand single file facing a wall, which is approximately 15 feet away. The first player throws a tennis ball into the wall, and then the second player fields the ground ball rebound. The second player then throws the ball into the wall and the process is repeated, with each player in line taking a turn.

If the player's skill level is low, the coach should toss the ball lightly against the wall. After catching the rebound, the fielder just hands the ball to the coach.

Coaching Points.   This is more challenging when players bounce the ball hard off the wall. Make sure fundamentals aren't lost in players' efforts to react quickly. Pay close attention to how fielders are approaching the ball.

Baserunning

Now let's switch to offense. We'll start on the base paths because good baserunning techniques are vital to a successful offense. And this is typically an area you'll need to work on with players, as young athletes often have poor running techniques.

Take the time to teach your players proper sprinting form. Teach them to run on their toes, to pick up their knees, and to drive hard with their arms. Make sure that their arm movement is by their sides and not across their body. Also, encourage them to run hard. You'll be surprised at how players gain speed just by being asked to run faster.

Running to First Base

When teaching players how to run down to first base, have them run through the bag like a sprinter hitting the finish-line tape, pushing down with the foot hitting the bag, throwing back the arms, and pushing out the chest (see Figure 7.19). Tell them not to lunge or jump at the bag; the only time they should slide into first is when a throw takes the first baseman off the bag, and they can avoid the tag by sliding.

Figure 7.19   Runner leaning into first base.

Baserunning Drill

Name.   **Approaching First**

Purpose.   To teach players how to exit the batter's box and make the proper approach to first base

Organization.   The coach places a batting machine on the field and lines up all the players at home plate with a bat. One at a time the hitters step to the plate. If the player hits a ground ball, he or she runs straight through the bag at first. If the player hits a fly ball, he or she should run in a flat arc to first base and run hard past the bag, looking for an opportunity to advance to second.

Coaching Points.   This drill helps ingrain in players how to start baserunning right out of the box. Remember they must run at full speed and always think a base ahead. Praise or correct players' baserunning decisions.

After hitting a ball to the outfield, the runner should begin a flat arc (see Figure 7.20). The runner should start about 6 feet out of the batter's box and hit the nearest left-hand corner of the base with the left foot. The runner should not slow down until after passing first base. On extra base hits, your base runner should continue the pattern of flat arcs to each base until running straight toward home plate.

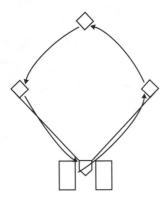

Figure 7.20   Running around the bases in a flat arc.

Taking Lead-Offs (Fast Pitch Only)

When a runner gets on base, he or she needs to know a lead-off technique. The most effective lead-off is a controlled lead. This type of lead-off not only gets the runner a maximum distance off the base, but it places him or her in a good position to get back to the base should the catcher attempt a pickoff.

To start, the runner should assume a relaxed stance by the bag with the feet no more than shoulder-width apart. The left foot should be touching the side of the bag that is nearest to the next base.

To initiate movement, the runner starts by taking a short step with the right foot in a direct line to the next base. Keeping the shoulders square to the infield, the player then uses a cross-over step with the left leg and arm motion to get a maximum, yet safe, distance from the bag. When he or she stops, the runner should come down with the knees slightly bent and in a stable position, the weight in the center of the body (see Figure 7.21).

Figure 7.21   A base runner stops with his knees slightly bent and weight centered.

Sliding

Base runners often must avoid tags at second and third base, and home plate; so it is important that you teach all of your players how to slide. Fear can be an obstacle for kids learning this technique, so be sure to start slowly and gradually work up to full speed. Sliding should be practiced only to the extent that players can execute the skill correctly, safely, and without fear. Here is the sequence of the bent-leg slide you'll want to teach players when they are ready:

1. Start the slide 10 to 12 feet from the bag.
2. Don't drop down to the ground—slide to the bag.
3. As you approach the bag, bend your knees (which will drop your hips). Then extend the right leg toward the bag and bend the left leg under the right knee to form a 4.
4. Slide on the buttocks, not on the side or the hips.
5. Tuck chin to chest to prevent banging your head.
6. Your extended foot should be 6 to 8 inches off the ground to slide over the bag.
7. Keep hands off the ground. Don't drag them across the ground as you slide.

Error Detection and Correction for Sliding

Young players first learning to slide typically crash into the bag, waiting too long to initiate the slide and then plopping down directly on their butts or legs. Teach them to slide early and to reach the base by skimming over the top of the ground.

ERROR	**CORRECTION**
Player keeps jamming her or his ankle into the bag.	1. Designate a spot at which the runner should start the slide. Because she or he is apparently sliding too late, move the takeoff spot farther away from the bag. 2. Teach the player to run harder and try to extend the slide across the top of the ground.

Sliding Drills

Name. **Support Slide**

Purpose. To show young players how to begin their slides safely and efficiently

Organization. Players squat on the ground, placing their left hands on the grass and putting most of their weight on that hand. From this position, players try to whip their legs out in front of them and land on their butt. As they get comfortable with this movement, ask them to land on their backs. Pay attention to the position of their legs, and make sure they tuck their chins.

Coaching Points. This drill is meant only to show players the basics. Sliding is easier to do at full speed; so as soon as they are not afraid to contact the ground, move them on to the running slide.

Name. **Slip-and-Slide**

Purpose. To teach sliding skills in an easy, nonthreatening exercise

Organization. One at a time the players run hard to the slip-and-slide area (a long plastic sheet) and attempt the slide. Encourage them to throw their legs out and fly through the air, as shown in Figure 7.22.

Coaching Points. Make sure players start their slide just as they reach the plastic. If they run on the slip-and-slide, they can take a bad fall and get hurt.

Figure 7.22 Slip-and-Slide drill.

Name.   **Game Situations**

Purpose. To erase players' doubts and fears about sliding on dirt by practicing the skill prior to playing in games

Organization.   During a regular game drill, offensive players, dressed in pants or protective sliding gear, slide in simulated game situations just as they would in a game.

Coaching Points.   Don't do this at every practice, but when you do, make it fun. And reinforce players who make good slides— whether they're out or safe on the play.

Hitting

One of the most difficult athletic skills to perform *and* teach is hitting. Before we help you with teaching the mechanics, take note of two prior considerations.

The first is bat selection. Young hitters usually operate under the misconception that the heavier the bat, the better. Help them choose a bat that is light and short enough that they can control it, because bat acceleration is an important key to hitting.

Second, don't limit players' hitting ability by encouraging them to just make contact. Positive reinforcement is important when they do hit the ball, but teach young hitters to be aggressive at the plate early in their development. You want them to get into the habit of swinging hard but under control. Teach them early to attack the ball with maximum bat speed.

Point of Contact

The old saying that players should "hit the ball over the plate" is poor advice. The only time to hit the ball over the plate is on an outside pitch. Pitches down the middle of the plate should be hit about 2 feet in front of the plate; pitches on the inside should be hit about 3 feet in front of the plate. By hitting along this diagonal path (see Figure 7.23) players can fully extend their arms, which allows for maximum power in the swing.

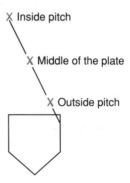

Figure 7.23   The hitting diagonal: contact points for a right-handed batter.

Now that you have an idea of what you are trying to accomplish, here are some fundamentals to emphasize when teaching your players.

Basic Hitting Fundamentals

1. Stand comfortably, with feet at least shoulder-width apart.

Error Detection and Correction for Hitting

While they are learning aggressive hitting, players often swing hard and at the same time move the head so they don't see the ball. Make sure that while the hands move quickly, the head stays still.

ERROR	CORRECTION
Player takes good cuts but always misses the ball.	1. Remind the player to keep the head still.
	2. Mark the seams a bright color and tell the player to call out the color as she or he hits the ball.
	3. Tell the player to bury the chin in the right upper arm and shoulder as she or he finishes the swing.

2. Stride 6 to 12 inches with the toe closest to the pitcher turned slightly in the direction of the mound.

3. Place the front elbow in a comfortable position, neither tucked in nor stuck up in the air. The front shoulder should be down, not blocking the view of the pitch.

4. Swing the bat directly to the ball.

5. Keep the head still and tuck the chin slightly. The goal is to look down the barrel of the bat as the ball makes contact.

6. Keep the weight of the body centered or slightly back through the swing.

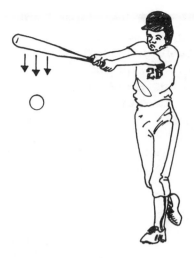

Figure 7.24 Batters should chop at the ball.

Inward Rotation

Inward rotation refers to the cocking action of the arms and hands made just as the stride is taken. Just before the swing, the arm closest to the pitcher should push the bat directly back, almost straightening out that arm. The motion is similar to that of a fighter who is about to throw a punch. Just before the punch, the fighter first draws back the fist.

Because young hitters may have trouble coordinating the stride and pushing back their hands, you may want to have your players start with their hands back and their stride out before the pitcher begins the delivery. The batter should swing around the hips throughout the hitting motion, keeping the weight in the center of the body.

Top Hand Hitting

The top hand is the power hand. Teach your hitters to throw this hand directly at the ball. In fast pitch, the shoulder closest to the pitcher should be slightly lower than the opposite shoulder. The head should be held low, with the chin slightly tucked to the chest. The head must stay still during the swing. Because line drives and ground balls make up the highest percentage of hits, teach your hitters to chop at the ball, rather than taking an uppercut or level swing (see Figure 7.24).

Slow-Pitch Hitting Adjustments

The same basic fast-pitch hitting mechanics apply in slow pitch. However, because the ball is pitched slower and with a much higher arc, slow-pitch hitters should take advantage of their additional reaction time.

Hitting to a certain spot (e.g., behind a runner) is much more possible in slow-pitch because hitters can make adjustments in their stance. For example, a hitter who is in a squared stance when the pitcher releases the ball can move the front foot forward to

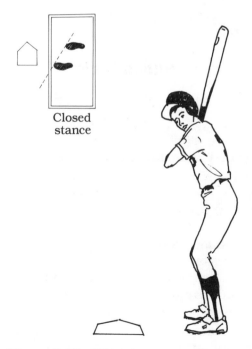

Closed stance

Figure 7.25 Hitter in a squared stance.

close the stance (see Figure 7.25). By doing so, the hitter can more easily hit the ball to the opposite field, if he or she is patient enough to wait on the pitch.

Also unlike the fast-pitch hitters, a hitter in slow pitch may swing level or even drop the back shoulder and uppercut on the ball (see Figure 7.26). Again, this depends on the game situation and the ideal location for the ball to be hit to in the field of play.

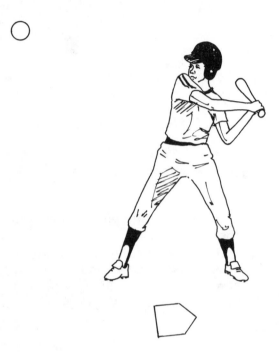

Figure 7.26   Hitter dropping the back shoulder to uppercut on the ball.

Hitting Drills

Name. **Fist Drill**

Purpose. To help players learn top hand hitting and inward rotation, as well as moving the hands directly to the ball

Organization. The hitter takes the normal stance, except he or she has no bat and he or she drops the hand closest to the pitcher down by his or her side. On command, the hitter makes a fist with the other hand and punches out at an imaginary ball (see Figure 7.27). The player should work on hand acceleration and hand movement to the ball.

Coaching Points. For younger players, you can hold a pillow or other soft object that they enjoy hitting. Pay attention to their

Figure 7.27   Fist drill.

weight shift. Don't let them hit off the front foot.

Name. **Hitting With the Hip**

Purpose. To teach players to keep their weight in the center of the body and to swing around the hips

Organization. Place a bat horizontally behind the hitter's back or hips. The player should hold it in place with the arms and back. On command, the hitter makes a swinging motion at an imaginary ball by turning the hips.

Coaching Points. Pay attention to how the hitter's feet are placed. Make sure the left toe is pointed slightly toward the pitching rubber and that the batter has a good base of support.

Name. **Batting Tee**

Purpose. To allow players to work on specific hitting fundamentals using a stationary object

Organization. Set up a tee and ball 10 feet in front of a fence. Remind the hitter of certain hitting fundamentals, and ask the hitter to concentrate on those aspects. The player should hit a number of balls into the fence.

Coaching Points. This is a great teaching tool, no matter what the skill level. Use it often before and after practices.

Bunting (Fast Pitch Only)

Teach every player on your team how to bunt. It's a great skill for making contact against a pitcher who throws hard; it's a good tactic for advancing base runners; and it's, at times, a good surprise strategy to get on base. But bunting needs to be practiced until each player has confidence in her or his ability to do it.

The best method is the angle bunt off the pivot. From the hitting position, the batter drops down to a bunting position as the pitcher begins the delivery. Teach your players to bunt only at pitches in the strike zone. Pivoting off the back foot, the bunter brings 75% of the weight forward on the front foot and moves the bat to a 45° angle, with the fingers protected behind the bat (see Figure 7.28).

Figure 7.28   Basic bunting stance.

Make sure the bunters keep their hands above the waist and cover the plate by bringing their left foot close to home plate. Teach them to adjust to high and low pitches with their legs and not the bat.

Young bunters will often shove the bat at the ball, causing it to rebound way into the infield. Teach them to let the ball come to them and to maintain soft hands. To bunt down the first baseline, players must push out the handle with the bottom hand. To bunt down the third baseline, players must bring the handle in closer to their body with the bottom hand.

Bunting Drills

Name.   **Reaction Drill**

Purpose.   To help players learn to move quickly from a hitting to a bunting position

Organization.   Place a number of bunters spread 4 feet apart in a semicircle around a coach. Players start in a hitting position; then on command they drop down to a bunting position.

Coaching Points.   Emphasize quickness, and stop each time to check the fundamentals. Later, go through a pitching motion so that players can get used to reacting to the delivery.

Name.   **Bunt or Catch**

Purpose.   To show young bunters that bunting is an easy task—just as easy as catching a ball

---

Error Detection and Correction for Bunting

Even after you tell your young bunters to keep the bat angle, they will often drop the head of the bat down when they bunt. This usually results in them missing the ball or hitting it into the air where opponents can catch it for an out.

ERROR	CORRECTION
Player attempting to bunt hits a pop-up instead.	1. Make sure the bat angle stays at 40° at all times.
	2. On low pitches the bunter should bend the legs rather than dropping the head of the bat.
	3. Work with players in bunting drills to keep the proper bat angle.

Organization.   A player in the batter's box faces a coach (pitcher), but does not have a bat. As a moderate-speed pitch is made, the player moves from a hitting to a bunting stance. After releasing the pitch, the coach hollers "bunt" or "catch," signaling for the player to make a bunting motion or to catch the ball.

Coaching Points.   Make sure the fingers of the batter's right hand are always pointing up. If the bunter rotates the hands down, it translates into dropping the head of the bat. Make sure the hands move up and down with the legs.

Name.   **Target Bunt**

Purpose.   To teach players how to bunt the ball to a particular area (used only after players master the basics)

Organization.   Mark a series of semicircles on the infield, and assign points to the marked areas. A coach tosses the ball to a bunter standing at home plate, and the bunter tries to bunt to specified locations.

Coaching Points.   Make this a fun game in which the bunter isn't just thinking about how to bunt, but is working on hitting the target. Initially, make it easy for everyone to be successful.

Common Softball Terms

assist—A fielding credit earned by a player who helps a teammate make a putout.

backing up—A fielder's moving behind a teammate to be in a position to stop the ball in case of an error.

balance point—The point in the pitching delivery where the throwing hand is at its highest point above the head, the glove-side foot is at its highest point above the ground, and the weight is in the center of the body.

bunt—A ball tapped a short distance down either foul line or in front of home plate by a batter attempting to advance a base runner or achieve an infield hit.

choking up—Moving one's hands up the bat handle to increase bat control.

count—The number of balls and strikes on a batter.

crow hop—Use of the body and arm in a throwing motion that generates maximum velocity on the ball.

cutoff—An infielder's interception of a throw from an outfielder or another infielder when no play can be made at the intended base or when another play is foreseen.

double play—A defensive maneuver resulting in 2 outs in 1 play.

drop step—A defensive technique that allows a fielder to approach a grounder or fly in the most efficient manner and retreat on those balls hit overhead.

earned run—A run scored through an offensive play rather than a defensive mistake.

error—A ball misplayed by the defense.

fair ball—A batted ball that is touched or stops in the field between the foul lines or that initially lands between the foul lines and beyond the bases.

fielder's choice—A play in which a fielder attempts to put out one runner already on base while allowing the hitter to reach base safely.

force-out—A putout on a base runner who had to advance due to the batter's becoming a base runner.

foul ball—A batted ball that is touched or stops outside the foul lines between home plate and first or third base, that bounces past first or third base in foul territory, or that first lands outside the foul lines on a fly past those bases.

full count—The count of 3 balls and 2 strikes on a batter.

hit & run—An offensive strategy in which the batter hits and the base runner steals on the pitch.

interference—An action by a batter or base runner that prevents the defensive fielder from making a play.

opposite field—The half of the diamond that is diagonally opposite the batter's box (for a right-handed batter, left field; for a left-handed batter, right field).

passed ball—A pitched ball that the catcher fails to hold or control and that the batter did not strike.

pick off—To trap a runner off base with a sudden throw and tag for an out.

pinch hitter—A player who is sent into the game to bat in place of another player.

pinch runner—A player who is sent into the game to run for a player who has reached base safely.

power point—The spot in the pitching delivery where perfect timing between the wrist snap and the hip snap results in maximal force on the ball.

relay—To return the ball from the outfield to the infield by using several short quick throws, rather than one long one.

runs batted in (RBI)—If a base runner scores when a batter gets a base hit, sacrifices, forces in a run by being walked, or hits into a putout, the batter is credited with an RBI.

sacrifice—Advancement of a base runner by a batter who deliberately hits the ball in such a way that the defensive fielders can only make a play on the hitter.

UNIT 8

How Do I Get My Players to Play as a Team?

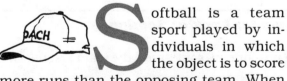

Softball is a team sport played by individuals in which the object is to score more runs than the opposing team. When teaching young people to play as a team, you must help each player define his or her role and how that player can work with teammates to accomplish common goals. The team concept is an important one, on both offense and defense.

Evaluating Players' Talents

We would all like to coach teams full of all-stars, but in reality every team has strong and weak players. By taking advantage of individual talents, you can devise an effective scoring strategy. There are a number of questions you can ask to help you evaluate your players:

- Who bunts well?
- Who hits for power?

- Who hits singles?
- Who can run fast?
- Who needs to play for defensive reasons?
- Who can pinch-hit or pinch-run?

The answers to these questions will help you determine your starting lineup. Although certain positions, like shortstop, require a strong defensive player, you'll usually start your best offensive players. After you have identified your best 9 or 10 players, it's time to put them in a batting order.

Setting the Offensive Lineup

There are no hard and fast rules in making a lineup, but there are some general guidelines to consider. Here are the characteristics you should look for when placing players in your batting order.

Batter #1	Speed, consistent hitter, good leader, good base runner, knows the strike zone
Batter #2	Speed, good bunter, good bat control, knows the strike zone
Batter #3	Best hitter on the team, high batting average, good RBI hitter
Batter #4	Power, great RBI hitter, good hitting fundamentals
Batter #5	Same as fourth batter but not as consistent
Batter #6	Good speed, contact hitter, similar to second batter
Batters #7, #8, #9	*Good place for clutch hitter or good bunter with speed*

Batter #10 (Slow pitch only) Smart hitter who can get on and run the bases

Rarely does a team have the luxury of having 9 or 10 great hitters. You simply have to look to get the most out of what you have. The lead-off hitter needs to get on base consistently, the second batter must be able to advance the base runner into scoring position, and the middle-of-the-order batters should be good, strong hitters who can drive in runs. At the bottom of the order, try to have players who can get the whole process started over again. Whatever the case, look for a winning combination and stick with it. If your team is not scoring runs, make a change.

Setting the Tone

Remember, success is not always rooted in physical skills alone. Attitude and confidence always play a role. For example, hitting is a difficult skill for anyone, and especially for kids just learning how to hold the bat correctly. Add to that a crowd of parents and peers and the pressure of a game situation, and the improbability of a young player's making contact with the ball increases even more.

As a coach, the worst thing you can do to a hitter is to give him or her 5 minutes of hitting instruction while the player is on deck, or worse yet, complex directions between every pitch. Encourage your players and compliment them just as much for a good swing or hard contact as you do for a solid hit. And encourage teammates to be equally supportive of a player at the plate.

Another important part of coaching a team is staying in touch with individual

---

Error Detection and Correction for Lack of Scoring

No matter how much care you may put into making up a lineup, sometimes the team just doesn't score runs.

ERROR	CORRECTION
Players are getting on base but not scoring runs.	1. Mix up the lineup to make sure those hitting the ball are grouped together.
	2. Use the hit & run (see page 63) to create more scoring opportunities.

players' feelings and perceptions. Some kids just love to hit lead-off, others prefer cleanup, and still others would rather hit at the end of the order, where they don't feel so pressured to get a hit. Players tend to develop feelings and beliefs about certain positions in the batting order and are upset when they are placed in what they consider an undesirable position. Try to sell your players on the important role of each hitter and help them to see that a strong team results only when everyone gives up a bit of individual preferences.

Setting the Strategy

After you have a batting order in mind, you have to determine what to do with it. You can choose any number of ways to run an effective offense. The following are four traditional strategies used in fast pitch softball to create scoring opportunities:

- Steal
- Sacrifice bunt
- Hit & run
- Drag bunt

Steal

Unless there are league rules against it, stealing is an important offensive tool that your team should use often. The best time to steal is when a runner has good speed, the catcher has trouble catching or throwing the ball, or the defense in general is not alert. Stealing a base is a great way to turn an average offensive team into an aggressive scoring machine. After a walk or single puts a runner in scoring position, stealing third even further increases the number of ways in which a runner can score.

If you have an older group, teach them to attempt a steal whenever they see that the defense is asleep. But whatever age you coach, teach your players to attack defenses, with the steal as a major weapon.

Sacrifice Bunt

Make teaching everyone how to bunt a goal for your practices. You need to be able to move a runner into scoring position (from first base to second base), and even the weakest hitters can be taught to bunt. Also, in younger divisions a multitude of mistakes can take place when an infielder attempts to field a bunt and throw a runner out. An average bunt can turn into an extra base hit that leads to runs being scored.

Hit & Run

One of the best offensive tools is the hit & run. When a runner takes off with the pitch and the hitter knows she or he has to hit the ball, it makes a tentative hitter more aggressive and breaks up the double play. Better yet, if successful, it also moves a runner into scoring position. This is not a play you can use if the pitcher your team's facing has little control or your hitters are too young or unskilled to make frequent contact.

Drag Bunt

If the defense is not alert or the first and third basemen are playing too deep, a good bunter may attempt to bunt for a hit. The drag bunt requires slightly different footwork from the bunting technique described on page 59, but the basic difference between the two is that a drag bunter waits longer to drop down from a hitting to a bunting position. Some kids have a natural gift for this, but most just need lots of practice.

Communicating Strategy to Your Players

Running an offense requires communicating with your batters through a signal system. Devise a simple one and use it in practice. Reading signals and executing an offense are just fundamentals of the game. Learning signals can be fun, like a new language, and it should not be perceived by your players as added pressure. Educate your players on what you are trying to do and why, so they can better understand what is expected of them. Have a sign for each play, such as the bunt or steal.

Teach your players that a sign stays on until you signal that it no longer applies. Have your players watch the entire series of signs, instead of picking up a sign and turning immediately to the batter's box; you may still be giving additional decoy signs. To make it easier, you can always give the ''real'' sign first. A typical signal system might include cues like these:

- Bunt—touch your belt
- Hit & run—rub your watch
- Steal—touch your nose
- Signals are over—clap your hands
- Previous signal no longer applies—rub both hands together

Offensive Team Drills

Name. **Performance Drill**

Purpose. To teach hitters to execute proper batting skills and base runners to react to various situations

Organization. A coach pitches with a batter at home plate and a runner at first. The coach calls certain situations, such as the hit & run, and then throws the pitch. The hitter must react and hit the ball; the base runner takes a lead and then reacts to the hit.

Coaching Points. It's one thing to talk about skills, it's another to perform them in a simulated game situation under some pressure. This is a good time to evaluate players' skills and performance in a game situation.

Name. **Signal Drill**

Purpose. To teach players to read the coach's signals in a simulated game situation

Organization. Place a defense on the field, but have a coach act as the pitcher. Another coach stands at the third base box and gives signals to hitters and base runners. Players react to the signals and execute the plays.

Coaching Points. This is an excellent way for players to develop confidence in reading signals. It also gives you an opportunity to see how players will react in game situations.

Building a Team Defense

Every time a pitch is thrown, the team playing defense must go into action. And when the ball is hit, every defensive player must fulfill a responsibility, whether it is to field the ball, accept a throw from another defensive player, or simply back up a position in case of an error.

Teaching team defense is very important and takes a lot of time with young players. You'll need to do it both on the field and in chalk talks, and you must give it attention in every practice. A series of diagrams at the end of this unit will help you learn and teach proper defensive movement (see Figures 8.1-8.22), but first here are some fundamentals of team defense that you will want to emphasize.

Defensive Backups

During the course of every practice, indicate where defensive players should be positioned and why. To teach players how to back up plays properly, use the buddy system. Tell your players, ''If Mary makes a mistake, then, Sally, you need to be there to help her out.'' In most games involving young or inexperienced players, it isn't so much the initial mistake that hurts but the series of mistakes that follow. For instance, a bad throw to first isn't critical unless no one is there to back up the play and the ball goes all the way to the fence. A single suddenly turns into extra bases.

Relays and Cutoffs

In addition to moving to the ball or to the correct base, relays and cutoffs are two very important roles in team defense. The middle infielders (shortstop and second baseman) are typically responsible for moving out to receive throws from the outfielders and relaying them to the appropriate base. The shortstop handles all relay throws from the left and center fielders, whereas the second baseman takes throws from the right fielder. When a deep fly is hit to an outfielder, the appropriate infielder runs out toward that fielder according to the outfielder's arm strength and lines up with the base to which he or she intends to relay the throw. For instance, on a ball hit to right field where the runner tries to make it to third, the second baseman runs out toward the right fielder and lines up for a throw to third. The weak-

---

Error Detection and Correction for Team Mistakes on Backups

Because the player to whom the ball is hit will not always field it cleanly, every player should have an assigned backup on every play.

ERROR	CORRECTION
Players stand around when the ball is not hit to them.	1. Make sure all players know where to move on any given play.
	2. Walk them through their repositioning for a variety of plays.
	3. Set up game situations that require players to react quickly.
	4. Make it a fun game by calling out situations and seeing who can get to their proper position the fastest.

---

er the outfielder's arm, the closer the infielder needs to get to the outfielder.

A cutoff player is one who gets in a position between the fielder throwing the ball and home plate. If the player intercepts the ball, he or she then either relays that throw to home or throws to another base to make a play on a trailing runner. The third baseman is the cutoff on throws from left field, whereas the first baseman takes all throws from left or center field over to right field.

Developing Pride in Team Defense

Everyone on the team needs to know her or his role in the team defense. You can help build players' pride in learning their assignments by praising players for their fielding and for being in the correct spots on a given play. Even your less skilled athletes can learn and execute this aspect of the game, and it should help them feel more a part of the team. Also, teach your players to talk constantly to one another about where they are positioning themselves, the number of outs, and who has responsibility for catching a fly ball. Communication is just another fundamental that brings a softball team together.

Defensive Team Drills

Name. **Positioning and Backups Game**

Purpose. To show players on the field where they should be on given plays

Organization. Place a team on the field and call out a certain game situation. When you say "Go," every player should move to the proper position. Cover every situation the team is likely to face. Talk about good and bad decisions and why players need to be at certain locations.

Coaching Points. Make this a fun drill, one that is run quickly with little standing around. Try to quickly explain "why" so players will understand the reasons behind what they are doing.

Name. **Relays and Cutoffs**

Purpose. To teach players the mechanics of relay and cutoff skills and to show them how they can help a team defense

Organization. Place a team on the field, and stand at home plate with a bat and several balls available. The play will always be to home plate. Hit a ball and have your players line up for the relay. Once they get the idea, you can have the cutoff person throw to another base on your command.

Coaching Points. The important thing is that players know where they should be and execute the relay and cutoff tasks. Speed is not important. Always make it a point to compliment knowing what should be done as much as actually being able to perform the task. Knowing what to do will always come before the ability to actually do it.

Defensive Charts

Figures 8.1 to 8.22 show a series of diagrams that break down team defense according to where the ball is hit and the number of outs.

Prepare players to handle their defensive responsibilities by working on each of the 22 scenarios in your practices. Correct and praise their efforts appropriately, and you'll soon have a solid team defense that responds effectively in most—if not all—situations.

Key

P	= Pitcher	3B	= Shortstop
C	= Catcher	RF	= Right fielder
1B	= First baseman	CF	= Center fielder
2B	= Second baseman	LF	= Left fielder
SS	= Third basemen		

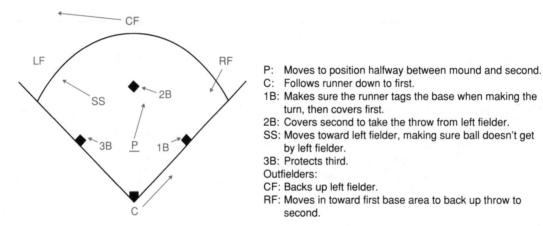

P: Moves to position halfway between mound and second.
C: Follows runner down to first.
1B: Makes sure the runner tags the base when making the turn, then covers first.
2B: Covers second to take the throw from left fielder.
SS: Moves toward left fielder, making sure ball doesn't get by left fielder.
3B: Protects third.
Outfielders:
CF: Backs up left fielder.
RF: Moves in toward first base area to back up throw to second.

Figure 8.1   Single to left field with no one on base.

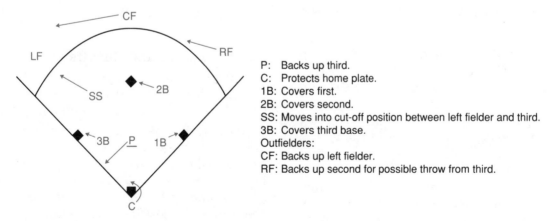

P: Backs up third.
C: Protects home plate.
1B: Covers first.
2B: Covers second.
SS: Moves into cut-off position between left fielder and third.
3B: Covers third base.
Outfielders:
CF: Backs up left fielder.
RF: Backs up second for possible throw from third.

Figure 8.2   Single to left field with a runner on first base.

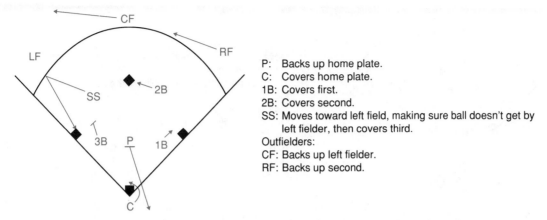

P: Backs up home plate.
C: Covers home plate.
1B: Covers first.
2B: Covers second.
SS: Moves toward left field, making sure ball doesn't get by left fielder, then covers third.
Outfielders:
CF: Backs up left fielder.
RF: Backs up second.

Figure 8.3   Single to left field with a runner on second base, runners on first and second, or bases loaded.

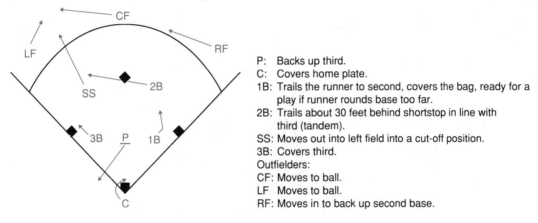

P: Backs up third.
C: Covers home plate.
1B: Trails the runner to second, covers the bag, ready for a play if runner rounds base too far.
2B: Trails about 30 feet behind shortstop in line with third (tandem).
SS: Moves out into left field into a cut-off position.
3B: Covers third.
Outfielders:
CF: Moves to ball.
LF Moves to ball.
RF: Moves in to back up second base.

Figure 8.4   Double, possible triple to left center with no one on base or a runner on second and/or third base.

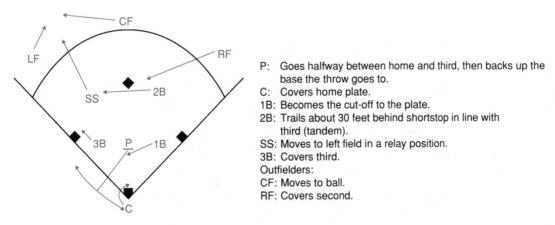

P: Goes halfway between home and third, then backs up the base the throw goes to.
C: Covers home plate.
1B: Becomes the cut-off to the plate.
2B: Trails about 30 feet behind shortstop in line with third (tandem).
SS: Moves to left field in a relay position.
3B: Covers third.
Outfielders:
CF: Moves to ball.
RF: Covers second.

Figure 8.5   Double, possible triple to left center with a runner on first, runners on first and second, or bases loaded.

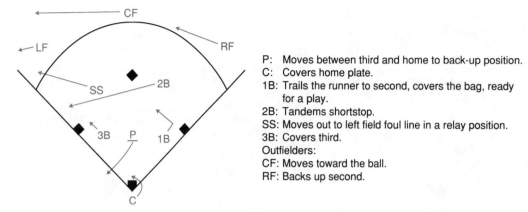

P: Moves between third and home to back-up position.
C: Covers home plate.
1B: Trails the runner to second, covers the bag, ready
    for a play.
2B: Tandems shortstop.
SS: Moves out to left field foul line in a relay position.
3B: Covers third.
Outfielders:
CF: Moves toward the ball.
RF: Backs up second.

Figure 8.6 Double, possible triple down left field line with no one on base.

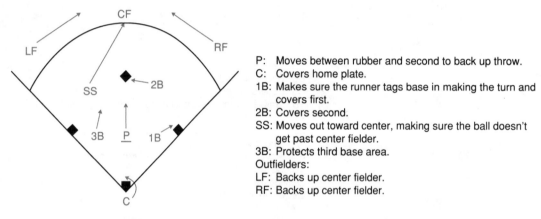

P: Moves between rubber and second to back up throw.
C: Covers home plate.
1B: Makes sure the runner tags base in making the turn and
    covers first.
2B: Covers second.
SS: Moves out toward center, making sure the ball doesn't
    get past center fielder.
3B: Protects third base area.
Outfielders:
LF: Backs up center fielder.
RF: Backs up center fielder.

Figure 8.7 Single to center field with no one on base.

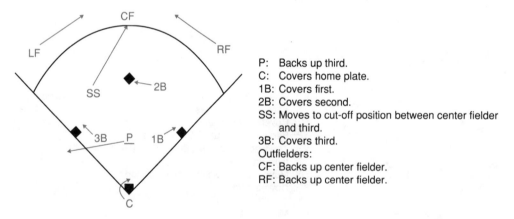

P: Backs up third.
C: Covers home plate.
1B: Covers first.
2B: Covers second.
SS: Moves to cut-off position between center fielder
    and third.
3B: Covers third.
Outfielders:
CF: Backs up center fielder.
RF: Backs up center fielder.

Figure 8.8 Single to center field with a runner on first.

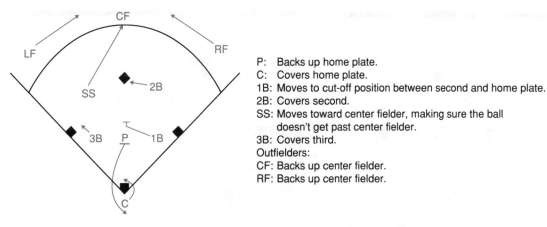

P: Backs up home plate.
C: Covers home plate.
1B: Moves to cut-off position between second and home plate.
2B: Covers second.
SS: Moves toward center fielder, making sure the ball doesn't get past center fielder.
3B: Covers third.
Outfielders:
CF: Backs up center fielder.
RF: Backs up center fielder.

Figure 8.9 Single to center field with a runner on second or runners on second and third.

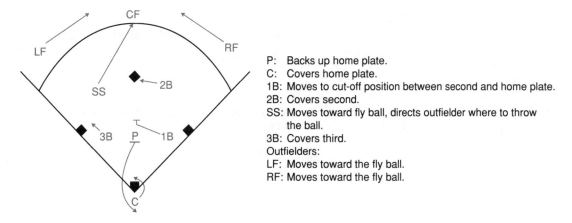

P: Backs up home plate.
C: Covers home plate.
1B: Moves to cut-off position between second and home plate.
2B: Covers second.
SS: Moves toward fly ball, directs outfielder where to throw the ball.
3B: Covers third.
Outfielders:
LF: Moves toward the fly ball.
RF: Moves toward the fly ball.

Figure 8.10 Fly ball to center field with a runner on third and less than 2 outs.

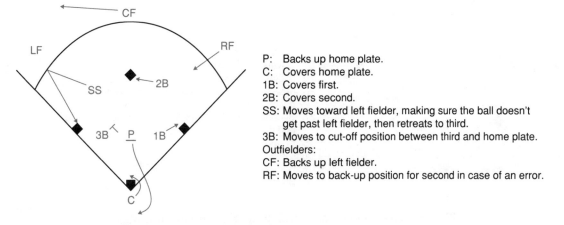

P: Backs up home plate.
C: Covers home plate.
1B: Covers first.
2B: Covers second.
SS: Moves toward left fielder, making sure the ball doesn't get past left fielder, then retreats to third.
3B: Moves to cut-off position between third and home plate.
Outfielders:
CF: Backs up left fielder.
RF: Moves to back-up position for second in case of an error.

Figure 8.11 Fly ball to left field with a runner on third and less than 2 outs.

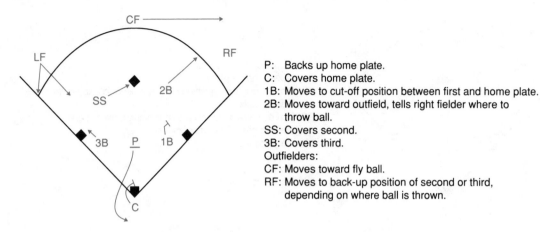

P: Backs up home plate.
C: Covers home plate.
1B: Moves to cut-off position between first and home plate.
2B: Moves toward outfield, tells right fielder where to throw ball.
SS: Covers second.
3B: Covers third.
Outfielders:
CF: Moves toward fly ball.
RF: Moves to back-up position of second or third, depending on where ball is thrown.

Figure 8.12 Fly ball to right field with a runner on third and less than 2 outs.

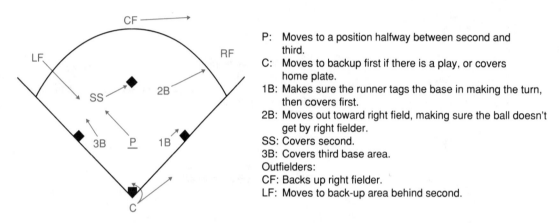

P: Moves to a position halfway between second and third.
C: Moves to backup first if there is a play, or covers home plate.
1B: Makes sure the runner tags the base in making the turn, then covers first.
2B: Moves out toward right field, making sure the ball doesn't get by right fielder.
SS: Covers second.
3B: Covers third base area.
Outfielders:
CF: Backs up right fielder.
LF: Moves to back-up area behind second.

Figure 8.13 Single to right field with no one on base.

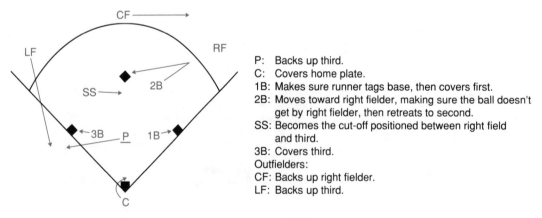

P: Backs up third.
C: Covers home plate.
1B: Makes sure runner tags base, then covers first.
2B: Moves toward right fielder, making sure the ball doesn't get by right fielder, then retreats to second.
SS: Becomes the cut-off positioned between right field and third.
3B: Covers third.
Outfielders:
CF: Backs up right fielder.
LF: Backs up third.

Figure 8.14 Single to right field with a runner on first.

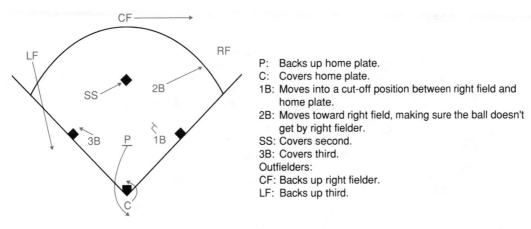

P: Backs up home plate.
C: Covers home plate.
1B: Moves into a cut-off position between right field and home plate.
2B: Moves toward right field, making sure the ball doesn't get by right fielder.
SS: Covers second.
3B: Covers third.
Outfielders:
CF: Backs up right fielder.
LF: Backs up third.

Figure 8.15   Single to right field with runners on first and second, or bases loaded.

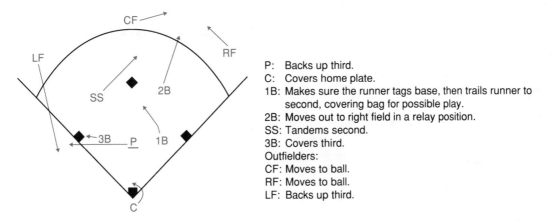

P: Backs up third.
C: Covers home plate.
1B: Makes sure the runner tags base, then trails runner to second, covering bag for possible play.
2B: Moves out to right field in a relay position.
SS: Tandems second.
3B: Covers third.
Outfielders:
CF: Moves to ball.
RF: Moves to ball.
LF: Backs up third.

Figure 8.16   Double, possible triple to right center with no one on base.

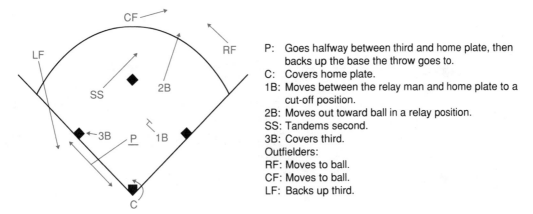

P: Goes halfway between third and home plate, then backs up the base the throw goes to.
C: Covers home plate.
1B: Moves between the relay man and home plate to a cut-off position.
2B: Moves out toward ball in a relay position.
SS: Tandems second.
3B: Covers third.
Outfielders:
RF: Moves to ball.
CF: Moves to ball.
LF: Backs up third.

Figure 8.17   Double, possible triple to right center with a runner on first.

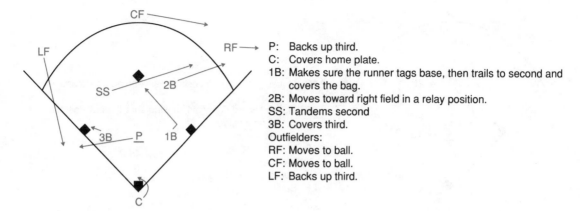

P: Backs up third.
C: Covers home plate.
1B: Makes sure the runner tags base, then trails to second and covers the bag.
2B: Moves toward right field in a relay position.
SS: Tandems second
3B: Covers third.
Outfielders:
RF: Moves to ball.
CF: Moves to ball.
LF: Backs up third.

Figure 8.18 Double, possible triple down right field line with no one on base.

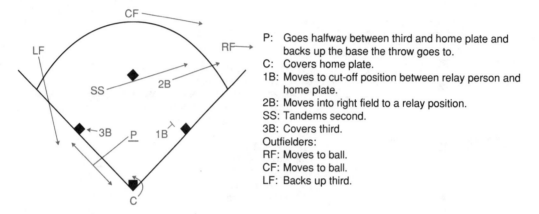

P: Goes halfway between third and home plate and backs up the base the throw goes to.
C: Covers home plate.
1B: Moves to cut-off position between relay person and home plate.
2B: Moves into right field to a relay position.
SS: Tandems second.
3B: Covers third.
Outfielders:
RF: Moves to ball.
CF: Moves to ball.
LF: Backs up third.

Figure 8.19 Double, possible triple down right field line with a runner on first.

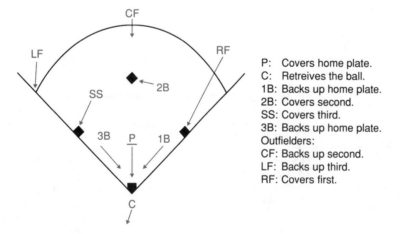

P: Covers home plate.
C: Retreives the ball.
1B: Backs up home plate.
2B: Covers second.
SS: Covers third.
3B: Backs up home plate.
Outfielders:
CF: Backs up second.
LF: Backs up third.
RF: Covers first.

Figure 8.20 Wild pitch with runner on third, first and third, or bases loaded.

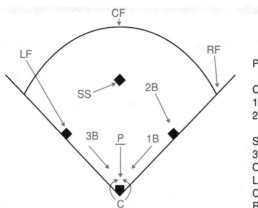

P: Breaks toward home plate, covering middle of infield.
C: Fields all bunts possible, calls the play.
1B: Covers area between first and mound.
2B: Covers first, cheats by shortening position (plays closer to first than usual).
SS: Covers second.
3B: Covers area between third and mound.
Outfielders:
LF: Covers third.
CF: Backs up second.
RF: Backs up first.

Figure 8.21 Bunting situation with a runner on first.

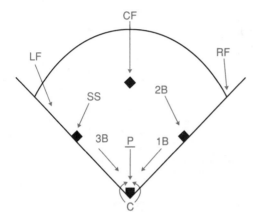

P: Breaks toward home plate, covering middle of infield.
C: Fields all bunts possible, calls the play.
1B: Covers area between first and mound.
2B: Covers first, cheats by shortening position.
SS: Covers third.
3B: Covers area between third and mound.
Outfielders:
RF: Backs up third.
CF: Covers second.
LF: Backs up first.

Figure 8.22 Bunting situation with a runner on first and second.

Appendix

Sample Season Plan for Beginning Softball Players

Goal: To help players learn and practice the individual skills and team tactics needed to play softball games successfully

T = Initial teaching time (minutes)   * = Skills practiced during drills and activities

P = Practice and review time (minutes)

Skills	Week 1 Day 1	Week 1 Day 2	Week 2 Day 1	Week 2 Day 2	Week 3 Day 1	Week 3 Day 2	Week 4 Day 1	Week 4 Day 2
Warm-up	T (10)	P (10)	P (10)	P (10)	P (10)	P (10)	P (10)	P (10)
Cool-down	T (10)	P (5)	P (5)	P (5)	P (5)	P (5)	P (5)	P (5)
Evaluation	(5)	(5)	(5)	(5)	(5)	(5)	(5)	(5)
Fundamentals								
Footwork	T (5)	T (5)	T (5)	*	*	*	*	*
Rules	T (5)	T (5)	T (5)	T (5)	T (5)	T (5)	*	*
Throwing								
Overhead	T (10)	P (10)	*	*	*	*	*	*
Snap			T (10)	P (10)			*	
Crow hop			T (10)					
Drills		P (10)	P (10)		P (10)		P (10)	
Catching								
Throws	T (10)	P (10)	*	*	*	*	*	*
Pitches	T (10)	P (10)	P (15)	P (10)	P (15)	P (10)	P (15)	P (10)
Fly balls			T (5)	P (10)	P (5)	*	*	*
Pop-ups			T (5)	P (10)	P (5)			
Grounders		T (5)	P (10)	*	*	*	*	*
Drills				P (15)		P (15)		P (15)
Pitching		T (10)	P (15)	T (10)	P(15)	P (10)		
Drills			P (10)		P (10)			
Hitting								
Swinging		T (10)	P (10)	P (10)	*	*	P (10)	*
Bunting			T (10)	P (10)	*			*
Drills			P (20)	P (15)	P (15)			P (15)
Baserunning								
Rounding bases					T (5)	P (10)	*	*
Lead-off			T (5)		P (5)	*	*	*
Sliding					T (5)	P (10)	*	*
Drills						P (10)	P (10)	
Team Offense								
Steals							T (5)	P (10)
Sacrifices								T (5)
Hit & run								
Drills								
Team Defense								
Backups								T (10)
Cutoffs								
Relays								
Drills								

Skills	Week 5 Day 1	Week 5 Day 2	Week 6 Day 1	Week 6 Day 2	Week 7 Day 1	Week 7 Day 2	Week 8 Day 1	Week 8 Day 2
Warm-up	P (10)	P (10)	P (10)	P (10)	P (10)	P (10)	P (10)	P (10)
Cool-down	P (5)	P (5)	P (5)	P (5)	P (5)	P (5)	P (5)	P (5)
Evaluation	(5)	(5)	(5)	(5)	(5)	(5)	(5)	(5)
Fundamentals								
Footwork	*	*	*	*	*	*	*	*
Rules	*	*	*	*	*	*	*	*
Throwing								
Overhead	*	*	*	*	*	*	*	*
Snap	*	*	*	*		*	*	
Crow hop	*	*	*			*	*	
Drills		P (10)		P (10)		P (10)		
Catching								
Throws	*	*	*	*	*	*	*	*
Pitches	P (15)	P (10)	P (15)	P (10)	P (15)	P (10)	P (15)	P (10)
Fly balls	*	*	*	*	*	*	*	*
Pop-ups	*	*	*	*	*	*	*	*
Grounders	*	*	*	*	*	*	*	*
Drills				P (10)				P (10)
Pitching	*	T (10)	P (15)	P (10)	P (15)	T (10)	P (15)	P (10)
Drills				P (10)			P (10)	
Hitting								
Swinging	*	*	P (10)	*	*	*	P (10)	*
Bunting		*	*	*	*		*	
Drills				P (20)	TP (15)	P (10)	P (10)	P (10)
Baserunning								
Rounding bases	*	*	*	*	*	*	*	*
Lead-off				T (5)	P (5)	*	*	*
Sliding					T (5)	P (10)	*	*
Drills						P (10)	P (10)	
Team Offense								
Steals	P (5)	*				*	*	*
Sacrifices	P (10)	*			*		*	
Hit & run		T (10)	P (10)	P (10)	P (10)	*	*	*
Drills		P (20)	P (10)		P (20)	P (10)	P (15)	P (15)
Team Defense								
Backups	P (10)	*	*	*	*	*	*	*
Cutoffs	T (10)	P (10)	*	P (10)	*	*	*	*
Relays		T (10)	P (10)	*	P (10)	*	*	*
Drills			P (15)	P (20)	P (10)	P (20)	P (15)	P (15)

Note. Because many skills are practiced simultaneously, a total time for practice is not given. However, we recommend that youth softball practice last no longer than 90 minutes.

Softball and Coaching Books

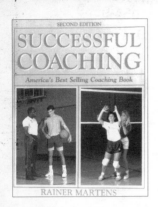

Successful Coaching
(Second Edition)

Rainer Martens, PhD

1990 • Paper • 248 pp
Item PMAR0376
ISBN 0-88011-376-6
$18.00 ($22.50 Canadian)

Revised to meet the needs of secondary school coaches and others who have a beginning knowledge of coaching, *Successful Coaching* is the most widely read coaching book ever written. It is a comprehensive introduction to the art and science of coaching.

Coaching Softball Effectively

Steven D. Houseworth, PhD, and Francine V. Rivkin, MS

1985 • Paper • 176 pp
Item BHOU0003
ISBN 0-87322-003-X
$18.00 ($22.50 Canadian)

Coaching Softball Effectively offers coaches more than just the basic skills found in typical softball books. This time-saving manual includes complete guidelines for teaching softball skills, and contains extensive daily practice plans and a seasonal plan for three age groups!

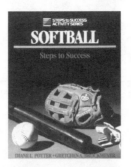

Softball
Steps To Success

Diane L. Potter, EdD, and Gretchen Brockmeyer, EdD

1989 • Paper • 228 pp
Item PPOT0358
ISBN 0-88011-358-8
$13.95 ($17.50 Canadian)

Teaching Softball
Steps to Success

Diane L. Potter, EdD, and Gretchen Brockmeyer, EdD

1989 • Paper • 256 pp
Item PPOT0359
ISBN 0-88011-359-6
$19.95 ($24.95 Canadian)

Softball: Steps to Success serves as a primary resource for students in beginning activity classes or as a self-instruction guide. Twenty-five steps (chapters) explain why each concept or skill is important; identify keys to correct technique; help players correct common errors; explain how to practice each skill in realistic ways; list specific performance goals for each drill; and provide checklists for evaluating proper technique.

Instructors need both the participant's guide and the companion instructor's guide to teach students effectively. *Teaching Softball: Steps to Success* follows the same skill progressions as the participant's book and features management and safety guidelines, rating charts for identifying students' skill levels, 104 drills to fit various skill levels, teaching cues to maximize learning, suggestions for identifying and correcting errors, and a complete test bank of written questions.

ACEP Volunteer Level

The American Coaching Effectiveness Program (ACEP) now provides two excellent youth coaches' courses: the Rookie Coaches Course and Coaching Young Athletes Course. The Rookie Coaches Course not only introduces coaches to the basic principles of coaching, but also teaches them how to apply those fundamentals as they instruct young athletes in the rules, skills, and strategies of their particular sport. This *Rookie Coaches Softball Guide* serves as a text for the course.

The second coaching education option at the Volunteer Level is the Coaching Young Athletes Course. This

alternative is for coaches who have completed the Rookie Coaches Course successfully and coaches who want to receive more instruction in the principles of coaching than is offered in that course.

ACEP encourages youth sport coaches to complete both the Rookie Coaches and Coaching Young Athletes Courses. We believe the combined learning experiences afforded by these courses will give you the coaching background you need to be the kind of coach kids learn from and enjoy playing for.

Human Kinetics Publishers, Inc.
Box 5076
Champaign, IL 61820

Place your credit card order today! (VISA, AMEX, MC)
TOLL FREE: U.S. (800) 747-4457 • Canada (800) 465-7301
OR: U.S. (217) 351-5076 • Canada (519) 944-7774
FAX: U.S. (217) 351-2674 • Canada (519) 944-7614